NEW CLASSIC
AMERICAN
HOUSES

NEW CLASSIC AMERICAN HOUSES

THE ARCHITECTURE OF ALBERT, RIGHTER & TITTMANN

DAN COOPER

THE VENDOME PRESS

NEW YORK

CONTENTS

═══

FOREWORD

ROBERT A. M. STERN

At first glance, the work of Jacob Albert, James V. Righter, and John Tittmann seems about as far from "cutting edge" as one can get. Yet in the context of its time—our time—it is radical, refreshingly so, taking its place in a broad movement of Modern Traditionalism, comprising architects who have decisively broken with the relentless present-ism of stylistic modernism that has monopolized contemporary architecture since the 1920s.

Modern Traditional work is backward looking but not exclusively or pedantically so. It is rooted in memory yet completely at home in the manners and mores of the here and now. In fact, it looks back in order to go forward, to add on to the culture, not to disrupt it. Modern Traditionalism embodies the "historical sense" that T. S. Eliot celebrated: that "sense of the timeless as well as of the temporal," that sense that makes writers, or in this case architects, "acutely conscious of . . . [their] place in time, of . . . [their] contemporaneity"*

The Modern Traditional movement that these houses so beautifully represent grew out of the conditions of the late 1960s and early 1970s, when Jim Righter, the senior member of the partnership, was an architecture student at Yale, then the epicenter of the "post-modernism" devolution wherein young faculty, especially the teacher-practitioners Robert Venturi and Charles Moore, proposed a simultaneous recuperation of the past and an embrace of popular culture as a way to reinvigorate the hypermaterialistic postwar modernism that had become complacent. In the hands of Venturi and Moore and their young followers, stylistic post-

modernism was irreverent and even sometimes silly, filled with arcane and even jokey references to formal tropes from architectural history and popular culture. A bit of that can be seen in some of the houses in this book.

With the passage of time, however, some of the young generation began to shrug off the teenage rebelliousness of post-modernist style and embrace a more scholarly approach to the discipline, taking each new commission as an opportunity for design research—research that digs deep into the evolved forms of the past, research that liberates the architect to go forward as part of history, and not against it. By the 1980s, when Righter was joined by Jacob Albert and then by John Tittmann, both also architectural graduates of Yale, the work began to resonate more and more with the authority of the past and not just an enthusiasm for it. This, in part, was the result of all three partners' increasingly unironic embrace of architectural history: to the stimulus of Moore and Venturi were added the engaged scholarship of historians Vincent Scully and George Hersey, also their tutors.

So much, however sketchily, for Albert, Righter & Tittmann's place in the larger scheme of things and how they got there. What is really important is the work itself, which I find refreshing in the grace of its erudition, lightly displayed, not flaunted. I admire the straightforward approach, the embrace of language articulately spoken in ways that can be appreciated by very many. I appreciate the inventive planning and the crisply articulated details such as window surrounds, brackets, wall paneling, and subtle moldings that, taken together, give each of the houses a poetic diction all its own. What a pleasure it is to have an architecture so beautifully naturalized—to site, to purpose, and to tradition.

* T. S. Eliot, "Tradition and the Individual Talent," in *The Secret Wood: Essays on Poetry and Criticism* (London: Methuen, 1920), p. 49.

OPPOSITE For Six Gables the architects developed a language of ornamented structure that defines its style.

INTRODUCTION

THIS BOOK PRESENTS an alternative way of making architecture, guided not by ideology but by curiosity. It should encourage us all to be open-minded and willing to learn from anything, old or new, high style or the vernacular. There is much in the history of architecture that remains meaningful and relevant. Albert, Righter & Tittmann show us how creative one can be while building on older traditions.

Houses should be built to last. But they should also be functional and beautiful. Permanence, function, and beauty are all necessary, requiring focus on both large issues and details. Beauty is perhaps the most elusive quality, hard to pin down and codify, though many have tried.

Jim Righter, Jacob Albert, and John Tittmann—the principals of the firm—and, I hope, the readers of this book share an enchantment with the architecture of many places and times. They have spent their lives looking at the world's architecture, seeking out what is beautiful or piquant. They build upon an architectural lex-

OPPOSITE Bold stripes animate the stair at Rocksyde.
TOP At Mountaintop House an axial approach draws you into an otherwise asymmetrical house.
ABOVE Checkerboard House is at first glance simple, revealing more complexity on further acquaintance.

icon that includes the likes of Samuel McIntire, Henry Hobson Richardson, and William Ralph Emerson. While the three principals love the past, they infuse its traditions with a new sensibility.

The first time I saw AR&T's portfolio, I was struck by the firm's sense of whimsy and fearlessness as they create new, original houses from past elements. They approach their projects as a single organism: their design process is an ongoing, passionate, and lively debate that can suddenly diverge in any direction yet always returns to a quest for an artful synthesis. Importantly, the houses of AR&T function; they may incorporate new directions in architecture, but fundamentally they have been designed to be enjoyed by their owners. All good architecture stands a test of time; a thoughtfully designed house draws upon our memories and appreciation of the architecture of the past. The houses of AR&T look back to this heritage of quintessential American influences to anticipate what I believe are new classic American houses.

Over the course of our collaboration on this volume, each of the principals articulated his approach to some of the core elements of architecture. Taken together, these statements may be seen to constitute AR&T's design philosophy, which is as fresh and irreverent—and timeless—as the houses featured on these pages.

ON HISTORY

JOHN TITTMANN: Architecture can be likened to a tree: it has historical roots and many branches, and the roots provide nourishment to the living branches. History is present, not past. Architecture, like a tree, is living. The branches of architecture—where we currently practice—are inextricably connected with its history, its roots.

JACOB ALBERT: Architecture relates to other architecture. We like Vincent Scully's formulation that architecture is a "conversation across the generations," and we like to think that we are taking part in that conversation, not repeating what has been said in the past but contributing new ideas in answer to what has gone before. The architectural movements of the 1960s and '70s were a great liberation from hang-ups about history. We shouldn't worry about our place in history or what is supposedly demanded by the zeitgeist. What we take from history (or from the present) is governed by our judgment as to appropriateness. The whole world and all of history are available and fair game. All of our design ideas come from somewhere. We may put them together in a different way, and even a subtle difference can be enough to register.

JIM RIGHTER: Memory is important; it puts you in touch with things that you have loved, some unspecific things that you have loved, feelings that you can't put words to. In responding to our clients' dreams and memories we enrich our architecture.

ON CLIENTS

JA: Architecture is for people, and houses should be livable. Clients spark ideas and set a direction. This is what makes each house different and special.

JT: Often, more than one style goes into the mix in developing a language that is particular to the client and the place. The house is a "portrait" of the client.

JR: Many architects can't wait to move on from residential work because their clients are difficult. It is just that difficulty that intrigues me. Sorting out the positions and coming to a resolution are exciting moments. It is very important to work long, and hard, and delicately, and forcefully, provoking the client to respond fully to this thing called architecture. The challenge is in creating delight. It is fair to say that your delight and my delight won't always match up. So it takes a great deal of listening and looking to understand your client's delight.

ON DESIGN

JR: Metaphor is a powerful way of starting, of generating a design. If the metaphor is good, I'm not sure that a mixed metaphor isn't better! I think of surprise as an essential ingredient in our architecture. Not a knock-your-socks-off one liner, but a subtle sense, where your expectation is either heightened or changed, or enhanced. For example, it is a great treat for me to have people visit our houses and to think they understand them from the outside and then to go inside and discover that there is an entirely different reading from their original assumption. You hire an architect to help you see life in a fresh way that you didn't know before.

JT: Creativity occurs not in the invention of a new language, but in the *inventive use* of language. Emily Dickinson wrote about bending the rules in a poem called "Tell all the Truth, but tell it Slant." She artfully bends the language as a way to express truth. We need the truth to be brought in slowly; we need the context of the standard, the expected. We can't just go straight; we need the slant and the bent rule.

JA: The style that results from a synthesis of sources may not have a name. The style is a way of relating the house both to the place and its traditions and to the clients and their tastes and aspirations. This book shows what we've done, but it is hard to make rules for others to follow. Most rules have exceptions, and the wonderful exceptions can be the most compelling. Artistic unity is thought to be a virtue, and it usually is. But disjunction or eclecticism can also be valid if done well.

ON THE ART OF ARCHITECTURE

JR: Function is homework. You get it right, and then what? It's the "then what" that is the architecture. Intuition is never written about in the critical press; it's too hard to talk about and unquantifiable. So how do you teach it? It gets into awkward things like background and taste. Since we don't talk about it, how can you judge it?

JA: In the absence of an agreed-upon set of rules, how do you know if something is done well? Instinct.

JT: We should measure architecture by its artfulness, by the skill of the making.

RIORS

ARCHITECTURAL STYLES

WE MAY SPEND most of our time inside our houses, but our first impression of them is invariably of their exterior. In the hands of a skilled architect, a house's appearance, whether historically inspired or contemporary, is composed of a carefully selected vocabulary of elemental details. Every detail is of concern, from the angle of the main roof to the type of hinges used on the shutters. The architect's ultimate goal is to create a house that is beautiful as well as functional, and his or her challenge is to honor both of these demands equally.

Albert, Righter & Tittmann's forte has been to reinterpret historical styles by updating and reinventing them, thus making these iconic forms their own. Unlike architectural firms that specialize in reproductions of old houses, AR&T's approach has been to use the past as a springboard. Their willingness to experiment with stylistic rules often borders on irreverence, yet results in a body of work that cherishes the past while avoiding being limited by it.

The principals of the firm try to avoid categorizing their projects by style, but they realize that we, the viewers of their work, need to do so as a means of describing and referencing each house. Thus, we have roughly grouped their exteriors according to style, even though AR&T freely and happily juxtapose and hybridize these categories.

PRECEDING PAGES The dormers at Island House point like ships' prows toward the view. OPPOSITE The classical temple front, as reinterpreted in wood by the American Greek Revival, is given fresh expression at Temple House.

CLASSICAL HOUSES

Classical architecture, inspired by the buildings of ancient Greece and Rome, has been a persistent and recurring theme throughout the history of European and American building. Classicism in America has taken a number of forms, from the Georgian of the Colonial period to the Federal of about 1800 to the Greek Revival of the early to mid-nineteenth century to the Beaux Arts neo-Baroque of about 1900 to the Colonial Revival of the 1880s through the 1930s. Classical design has flourished again since the 1970s.

Even though the rules of Classicism have existed for millennia, AR&T observe that their implementation has never been static. Classical elements may be used in a manner that does not simply copy what has previously been built but reinterprets earlier examples to create a modern version that is nevertheless in keeping with the spirit of the original style.

AR&T appreciate the American Greek Revival as "a translation of the most ancient and highly developed system of architecture we have into something an American carpenter can build. Simply by using columns and a pediment, you lay claim to a place in Western civilization and a whole host of associations."

The facades of AR&T's Temple, Rotunda, Riverview, and Farm Villa houses all have elements typical of the Greek Revival houses of the 1830s: a front-facing triangular gable, columns and/or pilasters (flattened half-columns attached directly to a wall), and an entablature (the massive horizontal beam supported by these columns). While the use of these elements fully respects

---

OPPOSITE The façade of Rotunda House that fronts the street is a variation on the New England Greek Revival temple front, while around the side a surprising rotunda, not traditionally associated with that style, signals the entrance.

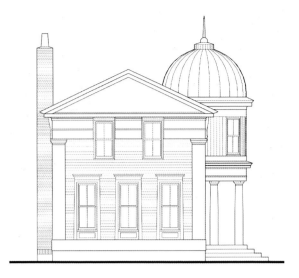
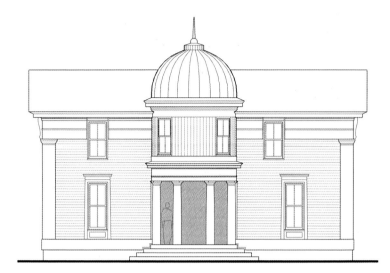

the principles of Classicism, at least in terms of symmetry, scale, and proportion, the architects manipulated or updated the composition to create a new version of Classicism.

For example, Rotunda House has a massive entablature and pilasters, and in keeping with the Greek Doric order, the columns and pilasters are constructed without bases. Also typical of this order, the first-floor window surrounds are battered like the door surrounds found on Greek temples. Then, in the manner of vernacular American Greek Revival, the second-story windows break through the entablature rather than residing below it. This is a bold move, as the entablature is visually the supporting beam of the gable. Moreover, instead of positioning the second-story windows in the traditional manner directly over the first-story openings, AR&T chose to place them above the spaces between the lower openings.

"The house becomes intentionally less symmetrical as you move from front to back," they explain. "The main façade follows the strict rules of symmetry, but, for example, the first- and second-floor windows no longer align above one another as you move back, and of course, there's the side entrance."

This placement of the main entrance not on the front façade but on one side of the house is a departure, and the two-story portico/domed tower confers a stately presence that perpetuates the Classical impression in a unique way. "The domed rotunda is Roman in origin, whereas a rotunda that is half-projecting and half-scooped out of the main block of the house is Baroque. We used this device to signal the entrance, which would otherwise be hard to find."

Another reason for placing the entrance on the side had to do with its impact on the spatial configuration of the interior. "If we had placed the entrance on the front of the house, in the traditional manner, the parlor would have been greatly reduced in size to accommodate the pass-through hallway to the back of the house. By using a side entrance, we divided the house into two discrete sections: a formal front half and the kitchen/family area in the rear. This is a relatively small house, roughly 2,000 square feet, and because of this layout, the occupants are able to move to separate areas if they so wish."

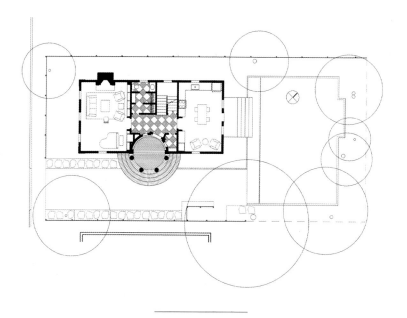

OPPOSITE, LEFT The street elevation is composed and symmetrical, but subtly quirky in the placement of the second-floor windows, which burst through the entablature and are not aligned with those on the first floor. OPPOSITE, RIGHT The side elevation becomes less symmetrical as it moves from front to rear. ABOVE The side entrance allows circulation space to be kept to a minimum. Generous living spaces in the front and back occupy the full width of the house.

With a temple front flanked by two shed-roofed wings, Temple House is more Palladian in massing, but it is rendered in a Greek Revival style. The first-floor window casings are painted the same color as the clapboards to suppress the windows, which didn't exist in Greek temples. "This keeps the emphasis on the colossal order: the pilasters, entablature, and pediment." As a result, the windows seem to recede into the façade, while the pilasters stand out as if they were actual full columns. "We like to use color as an architectural element; by carefully selecting whether it enhances or diminishes the contrast, one can achieve a variety of effects."

Further modifying the genre, the architects put a row of small, square transom windows within the entablature, in place of the usual metopes, or panels—a modern adaptation in the tradition of the nineteenth-century vernacular. This is a playful, but hardly naïve rendering: it is a thoughtful

deconstruction of the style and subsequent rebuilding of it. "We follow the principals of Classicism,

but we enjoy experimenting with it to create essentially modern architecture. This is more interest-

ing than the real thing, and certainly more relevant to our circumstances."

In their design of Riverview House, AR&T incorporated three Greek Revival pavilions, con-

nected by Shingle-style wings, to make a large house seem smaller and more approachable. "The

---

ABOVE With its tall, central temple front flanked by lower sheds, the massing
of Temple House is reminiscent of Palladio's Venetian churches, by way of
the eighteenth-century Redwood Library in Newport, Rhode Island. But the
architectural vocabulary is derived from the American Greek Revival.
OPPOSITE, TOP By replacing the expected metopes, or decorative panels, with
transom windows across the entablature, the architects depart from Classical
precedent. OPPOSITE, BOTTOM The façade gives no clue as to what lies behind. One
discovers that, in keeping with modern living, the kitchen is front and center.

three pavilions are rendered in different degrees of fanciness, depending on their function: most fully detailed for the living room (full Doric order, flush board façade) and simplest for the garage (no order, shingled walls)."

The choice of the Shingle-style connectors was judiciously made: "The use of a different style for the connectors makes the pavilions stand out more distinctly. We opted for the Shingle style and its characteristic gambrel roof to accommodate the necessary second-floor space while keeping the height lower than that of the pavilions."

Within the façade is a clever play on the Greek Revival vocabulary. Centered in its Neoclassical pediment is an ornamental circle. In Renaissance architecture a circular opening or window might have occupied the pediment, but here a solid disc, typically used as ornament elsewhere in Greek temples, appears in the pediment. Here, too, the single upper-story window breaks through the entablature, and the robust brackets on either side of it, when combined with the tiny square transoms, balance the three windows below.

Farm Villa combines aspects of vernacular Greek Revival Vermont farmhouses and higher-style Neoclassical villas. The tall, grand French doors, European windows, bracketed roof-rake overhangs, and almost severe regularity of the view-facing side place it in the tradition of Schinkel's villas, while the white clapboards used throughout and the plain, square porch posts, steep roofs, and more relaxed composition of the entry side relate to farmhouses of the surrounding area.

OPPOSITE The low-eaved gambrel roofs of the connecting wings
allow Riverview House's Classical pavilions to read more distinctly.
ABOVE Riverview House assembles three Classical pavilions with
shingled connectors. The level of ornament on each pavilion reflects
the formality of its function. Thus, the main living room pavilion on
the left is the fanciest, while the garage on the right is the simplest.

ARCHITECTURAL STYLES

In each of the above examples, AR&T have taken the fundamental principles of Classicism and boldly modified the canonical forms to adapt to the present day, while respecting the past. We recognize the Classical elements and symmetry, yet we are also aware that these houses are not simple reproductions. They are obviously Greek Revival, yet they are also unmistakably circa the year 2000. In lesser hands, these adaptations might have appeared cartoonish; it is a testament to the architects' love and knowledge of Classicism that they remain firmly grounded in the genre. AR&T aren't afraid of copying: "Copying is okay, but we're more interested in a transformation, even a very subtle one."

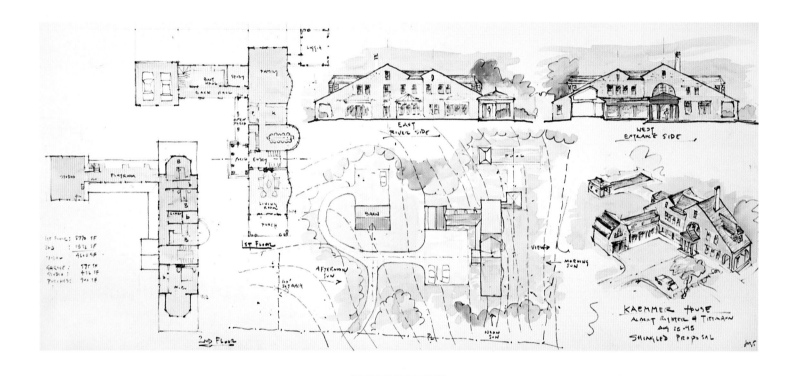

ABOVE Houses go through many stages in their design.
An early sketch of Riverview House depicts it as a large
shingled structure. But the L-shaped plan of the final design
was already apparent. OPPOSITE The second-story window
breaks through the entablature, an element that in Classical
architecture was traditionally inviolate. OVERLEAF Farm Villa,
like Riverview House, adapts high-style Neoclassical language
to wood construction in an American rural setting.

SHINGLED HOUSES

We often hear the term Shingle style bandied about, but what are its hallmarks? Merely covering a house with cedar shakes doesn't make it Shingle style: for example, many of the houses on Cape Cod are clad this way, yet few of them would fall into this category.

The Shingle style, as defined in the 1950s by the legendary architectural historian and Yale professor Vincent Scully, developed in the 1870s, as Americans began to look back nostalgically at their Colonial heritage. Architects examined the details and materials of early buildings along the New England coast (and more exotic sources as well) and applied them to a new kind of picturesque composition with an open plan, a horizontal emphasis, and a sense of billowing volumes clad entirely in wood shingles. The boundaries between walls and roofs began to blur. Interest in the Shingle style has been rekindled in recent years, as architects have again seen a value in reconnecting with these traditions and learning their lessons.

AR&T have drawn on the Shingle style for many of their houses, and it remains one of their favorites: "The Shingle style synthesized a wide variety of sources, just as we like to do, and arrived at a fresh and original formulation. This included American seventeenth- and eighteenth-century houses, the English Queen Anne revival, French vernacular manor houses, and Japanese houses. The style is endlessly flexible and adaptable to modern needs: it's a rational and sensible way to build on the seacoast, and it can be expressive and light-hearted." One of the reasons for the enthusiasm for this style is the informality of both interiors and exteriors and the relaxation of the

OPPOSITE, TOP AND BOTTOM A single broad gable organizes the façades of Penobscot Gable House and Gable in a Square.

strictures of Classicism, although it is not unusual to find Classical or Colonial Revival elements incorporated into the design of Shingle-style houses.

One idiosyncratic Shingle-style house, the Low house of 1887, has been particularly influential. In a move toward geometric simplification, architects McKim, Mead & White made the whole house one enormous, broad gable. AR&T employed variations on the theme of the Low house in several of their Shingle-influenced works, such as Penobscot Gable House, which borrows the broad frontal gable as an organizing, unifying device. "One virtue of the broad gable is that it accommodates ample room on the second floor while keeping the house thin—one room deep—for better views, sunlight, and cross-ventilation, as is appropriate for this vacation house on the New England coast. The geometric simplicity of the broad gable also promotes a strong, memorable image for the house. The windows are organized into horizontal bands that emphasize the horizontality of the whole composition and respond to the strong horizon line of the sea."

The façade of Gable in a Square is also organized into horizontal bands, but with two windows deliberately breaking the system to animate the composition and respond to the roof angles.

ABOVE McKim, Mead & White's iconic Low House represented
a shift in the Shingle style toward greater geometric order.
OPPOSITE Garden Wall House modifies the example of the Low House
by "bending" the main façade, throwing a kink into the overall order.

In this case, the detailing is even simpler and more geometrically "modern," with muntin-less casement windows. The big gable is a result of a geometric trick: imagine that a rectangular volume with a hipped roof has been sliced away, removing a large triangle from one corner. The result is a broad, gabled façade at an angle to the rest of the house.

Garden Wall Cottage uses but transforms the big gable of the Low house: "It departs from the Low house precedent by having a crook in the big gabled façade and a gentle curve in the roof line. Its broad frontal gable is in fact wider than the house itself, and the end of the façade that extends past the house shelters a garden. We placed big round windows on both the front and back gables to emphasize the center of otherwise asymmetrical façades."

A fascinating twist on the simple, broad gable is found at SeaBend, where the architects "broke" the traditionally planar façade, creating complex elevations and rooflines. This is an almost Cubist approach to changing the parameters of the single, all-encompassing gable/façade. "Here we started with the big gable and bent the footprint, or plan, while keeping the roof on the original orientation. The result is the creation of some unexpected and dramatic shapes that constantly change and unfold as you move around the house. This bend in the plan responds not only to the buildable area on a very restricted waterfront site but also to the directions of the best views. An addition we designed several years later keeps on bending and adding to the collage-like overlapping of forms."

OPPOSITE SeaBend's main gable is also bent, resulting in some surprising and exciting disjunctions when seen from some angles. ABOVE The architects enlarged the perceived façade of Garden Wall House by extending it, windows and all, past the end of the house to shelter a garden.

ARCHITECTURAL STYLES

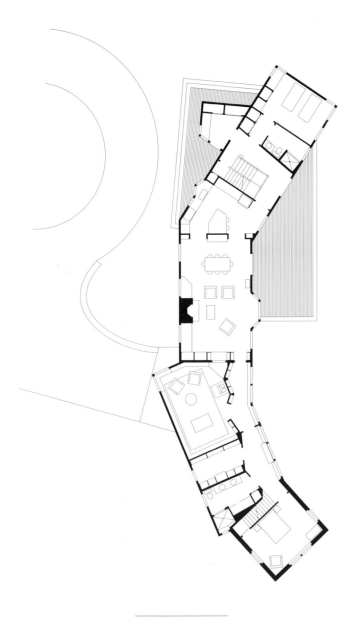

ABOVE SeaBend's plan is like a collage of overlapping shapes that respond to the limited building site and to the directions of the best views. Most of the plan is only one room deep to take full advantage of sun, ocean views, and breezes. RIGHT The ocean-facing side of Sea Bend is a complex, almost cubist reinterpretation of the Low House. The bend in the façade embraces an outdoor living space.

Not all of AR&T's Shingle style houses embrace the radical concept of the Low house. Indeed, many adhere to the more traditional façade massings found on late-nineteenth-century seaside architecture throughout the northeastern part of North America. One of the firm's more faithful Shingle-style renditions, Cape Tower House, features a horizontal emphasis, with gambrel roofs, delicate classical moldings, small-paned double-hung windows, and gently swelling shapes, such as the slightly bulging tower and the curved flare of the gambrel. "Another of the inspirations is Gunnar Asplund's Villa Callin in Alberga, Sweden, of 1915. You approach the house on axis, passing between two small pavilions, or gate lodges, which flank this axis and together with the house

form a courtyard. The formality of Cape Tower House is relaxed by the asymmetry of some of these elements: the main entrance, next to the tower, is off center; one of the pavilions (guest bedroom) is connected to the house; the other (garage) isn't. The garden/water side of the house is symmetrical, but its axis of symmetry is different from that on the entry side."

Mountaintop House combines some aspects of the Shingle style with the rustic trappings of a lodge at an Adirondack camp, particularly the large roof overhangs with exposed rafter tails and the many decorative details with a zigzag motif, including the rafter tails, the entry-porch post caps, the front-door trim, and the brackets both inside and out.

"Our clients led us toward the rustic camp imagery by stressing the woodsy hilltop setting, so unlike that of some of the old Shingle-style houses in their coastal resort community, which are right on the water. The house is perpendicular to the slope of the hill rather than parallel, which would have been the more obvious orientation. By presenting the narrow end of the house instead of its broad flank toward the arrival court, we

LEFT The architectural vocabulary of Cape Tower House is firmly within the Shingle-style tradition, although the axial approach between pavilions adds an undercurrent of Classical formality. RIGHT The plan meanders asymmetrically about a strong central axis of approach focusing on the stair tower.

ARCHITECTURAL STYLES

made this rather large house seem smaller and less imposing. In addition, this orientation gives more of the rooms and the outdoor living space a southern exposure."

Another of the firm's Shingle-influenced houses is Island House. Its pointy waterside dormers are loosely based on several McKim, Mead & White houses. And its conical tower, an example of the French influence on the Shingle style, references Henry Hobson Richardson's Stoughton house, among others.

ABOVE Unlike the entry side of Cape Tower House, the ocean-facing façade is fully symmetrical. The long porch and multiple dormers and gables open the house to the ocean views. OPPOSITE Decorative brackets give visual support to the overhanging second-floor gables, which are pierced by massive chimneys.

EXTERIORS
▲

Besides the Low house, another archetypal Shingle-style dwelling of the nineteenth century is Peabody and Stearns's Kragsyde, renowned for the complexities of its elevations and rooflines, and the manner in which it adapts to the terrain. AR&T's Rocksyde pays homage to this structure with a sweeping stone arch in a masonry foundation that extends a full story in height. "No matter how large or small they are, Shingle-style houses have an organic connection with the landscape, and the line between land and architecture blurs as they meld with their surroundings. We wanted to promote the idea of the house growing organically from the crags and rocks of the New England coast."

Another element of the Shingle-style vocabulary is the wide variety of interlocking gables that break up the long central ridge. The house combines Shingle-style elements with those of English architect Edwin Lutyens; the twin steep-roofed gables of the north façade bear witness to his influ-

OPPOSITE At Mountaintop House, the narrow end, rather than the long flank of the house, greets your arrival. ABOVE The house goes sailing off the mountainside toward the western view. LEFT Mountaintop House combines elements of rustic mountain camps and the Shingle style. BELOW Roof overhangs with exposed rafter tails contribute to the rustic camp feeling.

ARCHITECTURAL STYLES

ABOVE The entry side of Island House is a picturesque composition of balanced asymmetry anchored by a conical tower. The round tower and gently flared gambrel roof give the sense of swelling volumes characteristic of the Shingle style. OPPOSITE, BOTTOM, AND RIGHT The water side of Island House has a more regular order, with a row of four pointed dormers whose windows are angled to take advantage of the sweeping views.

ARCHITECTURAL STYLES

ence. Though fortress-like from some angles, on the ocean side the house opens up with an abundance of windows embracing the ocean view.

Japan, which opened its doors to the West for commercial trade in the middle of the nineteenth century, also inspired Shingle-style architects and designers. Harbor Cottage's elongated hipped roof with flared eaves has a Japanese flavor. "The house is a synthesis of many sources, which all come together in a new unity that can't

ABOVE Peabody & Stearns's Kragsyde, 1882–84, seemed to grow out of the crags of the rocky New England coast. OPPOSITE Rocksyde pays homage to Kragsyde with its complex elevations, stone base, and great arch. BELOW The bell-shaped roof of the study is another reference to Kragsyde.

be labeled; it has the flared eaves of a Japanese house, but it's equally inspired by Richardson's low, horizontal, hipped-roof train stations with their separate vertical towers. It also draws upon Frank Lloyd Wright's "floating" hipped roofs with exaggerated overhangs. Harbor Cottage appears to be Shingle style in its materials and its horizontal continuity, but at the same time it has a Gothic arcade and front door derived from St. Aidan's Chapel, South Dartmouth, Mass., and the rounded end of the roof over the arcade comes from William Ralph Emerson's St. Jude's, in Seal Harbor, Maine."

"The original inspiration for Harbor Cottage was Adirondack boathouses, because of its relationship to the water, but it didn't end up looking much like an Adirondack boathouse. It's a good example of how a metaphor that sparks your original thinking can transform into something different as a design develops."

At Harbor Cottage the hipped roof with broad, flared overhangs seems to float over a band of horizontal windows. The shingled wall below swoops down and extends out into the landscape to wrap around a deck.

Three of AR&T's works that share the broad, overhanging roof with Harbor Cottage are Secret Garden, Farmyard, and Winnepocket houses. "Secret Garden House is related to Harbor Cottage, but we nudged it toward the Adirondack lodge tradition in recognition of its wooded, rocky site on the northern New England coast. The rough granite chimney, outdoor fireplace, and exposed rafter tails and brackets all contribute to the lodge flavor. This is a house without a real façade. It's a space-defining grouping of pavilions and wings that you experience as you move around and through them rather than from a single vantage point."

OPPOSITE The multipaned, double-hung windows, the fringe of "shark's teeth"– cut shingles above the window, and the roof that sweeps around in a conical hood over the entrance all place Secret Garden House in the Shingle-style tradition.
ABOVE LEFT The broadly overhanging roof of the living room pavilion, with its exposed rafter tails, suggests the flavor of an Adirondack lodge.
ABOVE RIGHT The three wings of Secret Garden House meet at the tower.

ARCHITECTURAL STYLES

In Farmyard House, the architects introduced elements of farm vernacular, like the red board-and-batten barnlike entry tower, in deference to its Hudson Valley farmland site. The guest wing that adjoins the red barn tower slouches against it in a casual, shedlike way, further contributing to this idiom. The main part of the house, however, is distinct in form and style from these wings.

In the case of Winnepocket House, the voluminous hipped roof incorporates a second floor with a long dormer. "The tall roof seems to relate the house more to its mountainous site, whereas a more horizontal profile relates better to a seaside site, and the simple, all-encompassing hipped roof with a big overhang allows for undulat-

ABOVE LEFT AND RIGHT The tower at Farmyard House serves not only as the entrance but also as the hinge connecting the main house at the left to guest wing at the right. RIGHT The seemingly casual grouping of connected parts gives the feeling of a complex that might have evolved over time. OVERLEAF The voluminous hipped roof of Winnepocket House echoes the natural forms of its mountainside site.

ing irregularities, such as bay windows, below it." The entry to the house is marked by a slightly rounded protrusion of the roof. "We made the roof bulge out to offer more shelter for the entrance and to signal that the entrance was there. A curvy variation in an otherwise simple, rectangular hipped roof is an event that gets noticed." The bulge itself is supported by a carved post, a symbol of the rusticity found in mountain lodges.

ABOVE LEFT The bulge in the roof supported by a single rustic column signals the entrance and provides shelter there. TOP AND ABOVE RIGHT The all-encompassing hipped roof is the organizing element of Winnepocket House. OPPOSITE Bay windows fit below the large overhang of the main roof. In the dormer above, colonnettes form a layered screen that frames the view from the second-floor bedrooms.

EXTERIORS

▲

EXTERIOR

Details are the grace notes that animate a composition. They are usually related to function or structure, but they are also defining elements of style. Details can signal a known traditional style or set a new one.

Rafters do their workaday job of holding up the roof, but their ends, if left exposed, can be cut in a decorative shape that gives character and flavor to the whole house. AR&T have cut rafter ends in geometric zigzags to make Mountaintop House camplike; used rounded shapes on the rafters of the more elegant but still informal Secret Garden House; and turned the rafter ends of Family Camp into stylized boars' snouts, an image with special meaning to the owner.

Brackets, even if not absolutely necessary structurally, convey a sense of support and draw your attention to the underlying structural logic. The brackets under the overhanging second floor at Cape Tower House or the cornice at Riverview House, for example, give apparent but not real support. They make for a graceful and less abrupt transition between walls and overhangs.

Windows and their trim are key signifiers of style. A wide, double-hung window with the upper sash divided into many small panes says "Shingle style." The small panes visually continue the texture and scale of the shingles and contribute to the continuity of surface that is essential to the style. Even window surrounds can be an occasion for ornament. The job of casings is to cover the joints between the frame and the rough opening. But they can be plain or fancy, embellished with cornices above or brackets below to give added importance to certain windows.

AR&T have also explored the expressive possibilities of decoratively cut shingles; the many varieties of eave details; and the textural richness of stone walls. Every one of their designs involves the judicious choice of which details to emphasize.

TOP ROW FROM LEFT
Brackets beneath roof of wood shed at Fishing Cabin; gigantic keystones linking arched basement windows to upper windows at Keystone Cottage; zigzags on front door at Mountaintop House; living room window with "prow" balcony at Rocksyde.

MIDDLE ROW FROM LEFT
Brackets under oriel window at Lake Library; entablature with metope windows and brackets at Riverview House; roof soffits with simple brackets at Farm Villa; cut shingles and snout rafters at Family Camp.

BOTTOM ROW FROM LEFT
Barn foundation and sliding door at Stone House; roof brackets at Six Gables; window at Red House; zigzag rafter tail at Mountaintop House.

DETAILS

ECLECTIC/ VERNACULAR HOUSES

In nineteenth-century America, dozens of architectural styles and sub-styles coexisted and evolved. Some were carry-overs from the eighteenth century, such as the Cape Cod house, while others were part of a seemingly unending parade of Romantic revivals, including Greek, Gothic, Second Empire, Italianate, Stick style, Queen Anne, and Colonial Revival. At least one fashionable new style was presented to the public each decade, and often there were many variations on any given theme. AR&T have embraced this wonderfully rich and eclectic vernacular tradition.

An especially striking edifice, Six Gables combines the stylings of a French Norman château with some aspects of the Shingle style. "Our client liked images of steep-roofed French houses with exposed brackets and trusses, and although one can see similarities to the American Stick style, the immediate inspiration was French." Indeed, the house owes as much to the French Gothicism of Eugène Viollet-le-Duc as it does to McKim, Mead & White or Peabody and Stearns. The finish materials, however, are decidedly American. "The red cedar shingles, dark

OPPOSITE AND ABOVE The steep roofs, exposed trusses and brackets, and spiky pinnacles at Six Gables have the skeletal expression of both the nineteenth-century French Gothic Revival and the American Stick style.

green trim, and multipaned double-hung windows are more related to the Shingle style than to the French sources."

Lake Library draws on the Châteauesque style that was popular throughout the late nineteenth century. Note how the overall shape of the building is tall and clustered rather than low-lying, and sprawling. "This is a folly, a miniature castle, and the Shingle-style elements are squeezed

---

ABOVE The steep roofs of Six Gables sweep down to low eaves, helping to root the house in the landscape. Shed dormers are like flaps peeking up through the great expanse of roof. OPPOSITE, TOP AND BOTTOM Lake Library is a light-hearted folly, a cluster of vertical elements rising from a small footprint.

together vertically, erupting into a fantastical roof-scape of turret, light monitor, and chimney." The "Witch's Hat" tower and the secondary tower with its narrow frieze of clerestory windows are Medievalist conceits, embodying the Châteauesque style's preference for a taller, more varied profile than the hunkered-down rooflines of most Shingle-style houses. Particularly striking is the grand, two-story window that illuminates the entire interior of the house.

AR&T's Fishing Cabin comprises a unique blend of styles. It is a "Classical temple merging with a fishing shack by way of Sweden." If the architects' description seems confusing, consider that the façade was conceived of as a kind of rustic temple with tree-trunk columns and a pediment. "It's all made of flimsy-looking sticks, like the shacks along the Catskills stream where it's situated. The red board-and-batten exterior and its delicate scale are Swedish-inspired,

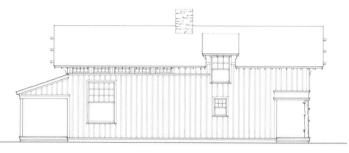

and the huge double-hung window on the south side, which is a big jump in scale from the other openings, is a hint that this is something more than an ordinary shack."

Farm Cottage, with its gambrel roof and flared eaves, plays on the characteristics of the so-called "Dutch" Colonial Revival. "The continuous eave line is more rigorous and modern than you would find on an old Colonial farmhouse, from which the style is derived. The piling up of three bay windows on the garden side is a fresh and unprecedented interpretation." Although located in the Boston suburbs, the house is in a farm setting. "Farm Cottage is an anti-McMansion, and is meant to look unpretentious and ground-hugging. The classical entry portico provides the only hint of the interior elegance."

ABOVE LEFT With its frontal gable and four tree-trunk columns, Fishing Cabin is a sort of primitive temple. ABOVE RIGHT The vocabulary of board-and-batten siding and thin, exposed rafter tails and brackets is more shack than temple. OPPOSITE, TOP Farm Cottage combines modesty and elegance. Its Colonial Revival imagery says "Home" while satisfying modern needs. OPPOSITE, BOTTOM A "pyramid" of bay windows on the south side puts familiar forms together in a novel way.

EXTERIORS

▲

For Mews House, the architects chose the Colonial Revival style to be in consonance with its neighbors. "The urban site had been part of the property of a grand old Neoclassical house, and we were intrigued by the idea that Mews House might appear to be an outbuilding belonging to the old house next door. Our clients hoped for a house that would appear modest and intimate, not loudly announcing itself on the main street. Our solution was to arrange the house in three connected, small-scaled pavilions that act as a wall between the busy street and a private garden. The central pavilion, containing the living room and dining room, is allowed to be a bit grander than the others on the garden side, with a classical portico and full-length shutters that make the windows look taller. Because they are proportioned like doors, the tall shutters also impart a greater sense of a garden pavilion."

AR&T designed Stone House as a variation on the indigenous masonry farmhouses of Pennsylvania. "The Pennsylvania farmhouse image came from our clients, who, though they have lived in the Boston suburbs for years, grew up around Philadelphia. The stone was brought from Chester

County and a Pennsylvania mason went up to the Boston area to instruct the local masons in Pennsylvanian techniques, which included slathering on lots of mortar." The wide clapboards of the wood-clad side wings are an authentic element of Pennsylvania farmhouses, as are the pent eaves and the entry-porch roof without posts. "We combined these farmhouse elements with characteristics of the country house: a greater generosity of spaces, bigger windows, more elegant interior detailing, and the slightly grand gesture of the curved bay window, on center, with floor-to-ceiling double-hung windows."

OPPOSITE The three connected pavilions of Mews House wrap around a private garden, a serene and protected oasis in an urban neighborhood. TOP The quiet, subtle monochrome palette of the exterior is enlivened by Chinese red window sashes. The details are Colonial Revival, but there is no specific precedent for the composition of the house as a whole. BOTTOM Dividing Mews House into three pavilions reduces its scale and conspicuousness on the main street.

Island Hill House is based in the Colonial Revival but develops a special blend prompted by the client. "We call it Nantucket meets Williamsburg. It has the simple, gabled, shingled blocks with 6-over-6 or 6-over-1 windows found on Nantucket, and the steep roofs and narrow vertical dormers of Williamsburg." Composed as a set of connected pavilions to lessen the scale of the entire complex, Island Hill House is generally symmetrical but not rigidly so. A tall central pavilion with a cupola resembles a public building, such as a meeting house or town hall, but it is actually a single, high-ceilinged

LEFT Stone House is a careful study in the architectural vocabulary of rural Pennsylvania, with its rough stone walls, wide clapboard siding, and pent eaves. ABOVE The somewhat freewheeling arrangement of windows on the entry side has a vernacular flavor and reveals little about the spaces within.

room containing living and dining areas. Low "hyphens" connect the central pavilion to story-and-a-half "houses."

In all of these houses, there are obvious historical influences for the architecture, yet AR&T finesse the tenets of each style, varying them slightly to signal that these dwellings are not mere reproductions. The secret is in the judicious play on the elements, which are slightly exaggerated or modified. The onlooker knows immediately what style the house is, but there's just enough of a twist to make him or her second-guess their assumptions and realize how innovative it is.

ABOVE The center pavilion of Island Hill House looks like a two-and-a-half story building but in fact is one big, open space, lit by a cupola, housing the living and dining areas. The entrance is in the "hyphen" between this pavilion on the left and a bedroom wing on the right. OPPOSITE The kitchen occupies the hyphen to the left of the living/dining pavilion and is rendered on the exterior as an arcade that has been enclosed. The roofs fold and intersect in a way that locks the whole rambling composition together.

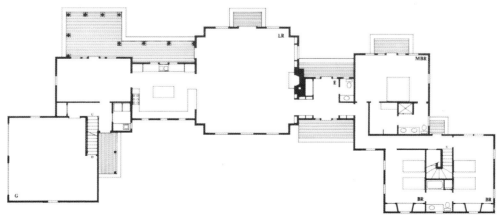

TRANSITIONAL

AR&T's roots are in the late 1960s and early 1970s, a period of transition from the Modern movement to a greater appreciation of history. A hunger for meaning and a recognition of the power of the associations inherent in traditional house forms led to the reappearance of pitched roofs in place of flat ones, windows instead of walls of glass, and ornament as an antidote to abstraction. "The embrace of these older traditions was gradual, as we learned the language."

Early AR&T houses incorporate traditional house forms while playing with abstract geometries. Several are based on the square, rotating or eroding it. Traditional forms such as hipped roofs and vertically proportioned windows are introduced. But the details are simple: minimal trim and no muntins dividing the windows.

In Monitor House, a small, simple plywood-clad summer cottage, there are echoes of Palladio's Villa Rotunda, a square plan with a central dome. In an abstracted way Tower House captures some of the spirit of the Victorian house that had once stood on the site. At Cube House ornament appears in the form of a band of cut shingles. Atrium House, an unbuilt project, inverts the hipped roof of the other three with shed roofs that slope down toward the central courtyard in the manner of an ancient Roman house. The courtyard, in turn, spills down at one corner with Baroque dynamism to a lap pool that penetrates the perimeter walls of the square plan

1. Monitor House: The square plan with a hipped roof is carved away at two of the corners and at the entry. The square establishes an overall order that remains despite these several deformations.

2. Cube House also starts with a square, but one corner of the ground floor is carved away for a recessed entry, and one quadrant of the second floor is carved away for an open deck.

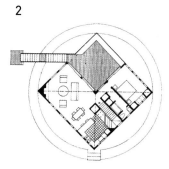

3. Atrium House is inward-looking, incorporating outdoor living space within the square volume. It looks to Mediterranean and Latin American houses, with a lively courtyard contained within a plain, undemonstrative shell.

4. Tower House consists of two squares connected by an arcade, the larger for the main house, the smaller for the garage/studio. The main house is actually a square within a square, the inner square rising to a height of three stories.

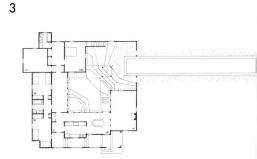

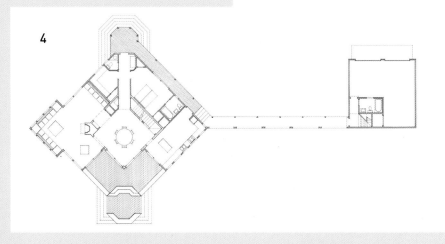

HOUSES

INNOVATIVE/ WHIMSICAL HOUSES

And then there are those houses that have distinct traces of and references to historical styles, yet simultaneously avoid being thrust into the "contemporary" or "modern" genre. As a firm known for experimenting with historical fundamentals, AR&T have produced several works that fall into this type. While fully mindful of tradition and precedent, their playful and creative minds cannot help but pose the question, "What would happen if we . . ." Thus fanciful permutations on themes spring to life.

Checkerboard House, located in Cambridge, MA, draws upon an eclectic mix of sources. At first glance, its most distinguishing feature is the black-and-gray diamond pattern decorating the second story. These are asphalt shingles, a material that was originally intended as an inexpensive fix for exterior siding in need of an upgrade. The false-fronted flat cornice is embellished with swags. Behind this façade, the asymmetrical shed roof is pitched to drain water away from the attached house next door. "The asphalt shingles and vinyl siding undercut the pretentiousness of the square, fluted Doric columns and swags, while the columns and swags elevate the asphalt and vinyl beyond their usual tackiness. The checkerboard pattern of shingles recalls such monuments as the Doge's Palace in Venice, but it is also like some houses around the corner."

OPPOSITE The "false front" of Checkerboard House presents a striking and memorable image to the street. It adopts the flat cornice line shared by a number of nearby buildings while allowing the shed roof behind to drain its rainwater to the side as necessary. ABOVE The earliest design sketch shows the checkerboard pattern on the façade, which makes a bold statement with the simplest of means.

ARCHITECTURAL STYLES

▲

Far away from the urban milieu, we find a truly whimsical structure: Pinwheel House. In past centuries, it was not at all unusual for the owner of a country estate to commission a folly, that is, a smaller, usually ornamental outbuilding that may have had little or nothing to do with the architectural style of the main house and was intended to be viewed from the house or grounds as a nostalgic diversion. Often executed in the form of a ruined abbey or similar antiquity, follies were quirky features that enhanced the landscape. AR&T's Pinwheel House falls squarely within the spirit of such a place. It is a guest house that belongs to a house that is itself a folly, a three-story tower.

"Pinwheel House is a composition of familiar parts put together in surprising ways: normal double-hung windows that are graduated in size to accommodate the slope of the roofs below them; mooring balls that are fitted with light bulbs to serve as lanterns; a normal hipped roof that is rotated 45 degrees to create its jester's-cap look. The house possesses a rigorously consistent geometry that produces a whimsical effect." The saw-tooth shed additions on each side and the graduated series of windows accentuate the playfulness of the building. Pinwheel House defies stylistic labeling, but it fits comfortably in its New England seaside setting.

TOP AND ABOVE Pinwheel House's main room serves as a living room for the guest house during the summer season and a garage in the winter. OPPOSITE In the design of the unusual main roof, a simple, square, hipped roof is rotated 45 degrees with respect to the second-floor plan. At the hips, which would normally rest on the corners of the building, dangling mooring balls fitted with light bulbs glow at night.

TOWERS

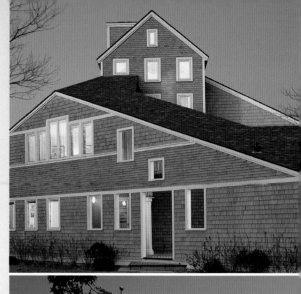

One of AR&T's favorite architectural features is the tower. Towers capture the imagination because we picture ourselves in them, surveying the scene from a safe perch. They call up romantic associations with medieval castles. They also convey the imagery of lighthouses, windmills, tree houses, and silos. This imagery may connect them to traditions of their place or express a favorite fantasy of their owner.

Towers can be part of larger buildings or freestanding. AR&T designed a whole house on an island in Maine in the form of a three-story tower with the living room on top to maximize the views for the occupants during daylight hours. When integrated into a building, a tower is often used as a device to contain the stairway, and thus provides vertical circulation between the floors. Or it might have a room at the top for enjoying a wonderful view. Sometimes the top of the tower can resemble a miniature house set tantalizingly high above the ground. A tower may also be used to signal the building's entrance, whether in the base of the tower itself or adjacent to it.

Visually, towers can serve as a compositional tool, creating a vertical foil to lower, horizontal parts of the building and contributing interest and variety to the building's silhouette.

TOP ROW FROM LEFT

Gable in a Square: The tower is a small house on top of the big house. Island House: A band of windows wraps around the tower, tying it to the adjacent dormer. Farmyard House: The tower connects two wings. Ferguson Museum: The tower signals the entrance.

MIDDLE ROW FROM LEFT

Cape Tower House: A subtle bulge animates this tower. Pasture House: The tower points toward the view.

BOTTOM ROW FROM LEFT

Hillside House: The tower links five floor levels. Cape Courtyard House: The tower is distinguished by a different color. SeaBend: The tower's battered walls brace it against the ocean storms. Island Tower House: The whole house is a tower.

COURTYARDS, ENTRANCES, AND PORCHES

A house is just one part of the overall design of its site. "We often think of our houses as pavilions in a garden, and we're designing the whole garden." The house must relate not only to its immediate surroundings but also to the entire visible environment. "The design of a house is shaped in the most basic way by its relationship to the road, the terrain, the view, the sun, and other buildings. The house, in turn, inevitably reshapes the landscape in some way."

Entrances, porches, and courtyards are transitional elements that help connect a house to its surroundings and form part of the experience of moving between outside and inside. Porches and courtyards can serve both as places of arrival and as outdoor living spaces. "Each of these functions enriches one's enjoyment of the site and augments the usable space of the house."

OPPOSITE Mountaintop House's living porch takes
the best possible advantage of the surrounding
vistas, which can be enjoyed rain or shine.

COURTYARDS

Courtyards are outdoor rooms, and just as important as interior ones. They can be shaped by wrapping the house around them or by flanking the house with outbuildings or garden walls to define a space. Courtyards give privacy to outdoor activities in an urban context or protection from the wilds of nature in a rural setting. "They tame nature while still allowing you to participate in it."

The courtyard of Cape Tower House is a place of arrival, giving you the feeling you've entered somewhere special and surrounding you in a warm embrace. For this house on the coast, the courtyard also provides a sheltered spot for a garden that is open to the southern sun but shielded from the wind. As you enter the courtyard and face the stair tower of the house, you can see that the courtyard is flanked on one side by a one-story wing of guest bedrooms and on the other by a separate garage. The matching lantern cupolas on the roofs of the garage and guest wing are like gateposts to the courtyard.

Riverview House also has an arrival court, defined by the L-shaped house on two sides and a separate barn on a third. The approach is orchestrated in such a way that you reach the courtyard without seeing the river, the view of which unfolds dramatically once you've entered the house. The grouping of connected and separate pavilions around the courtyard resembles a village that might have evolved over time. Composing this large house as a collection of smaller pavilions makes it friendly and approachable rather than imposing.

OPPOSITE, TOP The courtyard of Cape Tower House is a welcoming place of arrival and a sheltered garden, protected from prevailing winds but open to the southern sun. OPPOSITE, BOTTOM At Riverview House three gabled façades—the barn/studio, the living room, and the garage—form the three sides of the arrival courtyard, which is reached at the end of a long, winding driveway.

ABOVE At Cape Courtyard House a sheltered, sunny garden is also
part of the entry sequence. From the entry portico, one traverses the
colonnade, experiencing the courtyard, before entering the house
through the base of the tower. OPPOSITE The ruins of an old barn
foundation were incorporated into Farmyard House's courtyard.

EXTERIORS

▲

Cape Courtyard House is another village-like grouping around an outdoor space. The parts, like those of Riverview House, are distinguished by color and by height: one- and two-story wings are juxtaposed to a tower. The low wing containing the entry portico acts as a screen between the driveway/parking area and the courtyard while admitting sunlight from the south. As at Cape Tower House, the courtyard provides a sunny place out of the wind.

Sometimes AR&T use existing architectural features to augment new construction in creating a courtyard. At Farmyard House the ruins of an old barn foundation were incorporated into one side of the farmyard, and new buildings were grouped around two other sides to define an arrival court. The main house presents a private face to the courtyard but opens up on the other side, where expansive bay windows command a sweeping view of a pond in the middle distance and rolling hills beyond.

Secret Garden House embraces a courtyard that is part of an entry sequence but also functions as an intimate outdoor living space. Surrounded on two sides by wings of the house and on the other two sides by shingled walls, the garden is lush with indigenous Maine plants that are safely out of bounds to marauding deer.

ABOVE Secret Garden House incorporates a completely enclosed courtyard protected from deer. Access is gained through what appears to be the front door, which actually opens onto a colonnade that leads to the true entry. OPPOSITE After passing through this doorway, a visitor enters an intimate outdoor living area and garden.

EXTERIORS

▲

ENTRY PORCHES

Great architecture of the past, both high style and vernacular, often made a ceremony of the process of entering a building. AR&T believe in the ceremonial value of an entrance and in the idea of emphasis. An interesting and memorable composition often establishes a hierarchy of importance, with some elements played up more than others. Budgets also demand that you refrain from making everything fancy and concentrate the fanciness in just a few places. The entrance is usually one of those places. The approach to a house is a key part of the design, setting the stage for the whole experience. An entry porch enhances the approach in several ways: it's a sign of welcome; it provides shelter from the elements; it is an occasion for ornament; and it is a place to announce a style.

Some of AR&T's entry porches project out from the body of the house, while others are carved from it. "A variety of factors, including both spatial considerations and style, influence the choice of one type or the other." Among the examples of the latter type is the entrance of Garden Wall Cottage, where the walls around the front door gently push back behind the plane of the façade, under a wide, sweeping arch. The arch is embellished with cut shingles that further celebrate the entrance. The recessed entry is one element of a highly dynamic composition: the door is set back, the arch pushes up, and the deck curves outward.

At SeaBend the entry seems to pivot out as a triangular flap from the façade, and this triangle is then carved away to create a recessed porch. At Checkerboard House the porch columns are like a screen in the plane of the façade, behind which the entry porch is hollowed out. Inside the

OPPOSITE The entry to Garden Wall Cottage is subtly
recessed into the façade and sheltered under a broad
arch that is ornamented with cut shingles.

ABOVE LEFT The new porch at Stable House gives a simple but proper entrance to an old house that had been converted from a horse barn. ABOVE RIGHT The portico of Cape Courtyard House ushers you into the courtyard and screens it from the parking area. RIGHT In keeping with the dynamic geometry of SeaBend, a covered porch is carved from the entry, which is like a wedge that pivots from the main façade. OPPOSITE, LEFT Stone House's portico is a cantilevered pent roof, an indigenous element of rural Pennsylvania houses. OPPOSITE, RIGHT Emphasis is given to the entry at Farm Cottage with an elegant Colonial Revival portico.

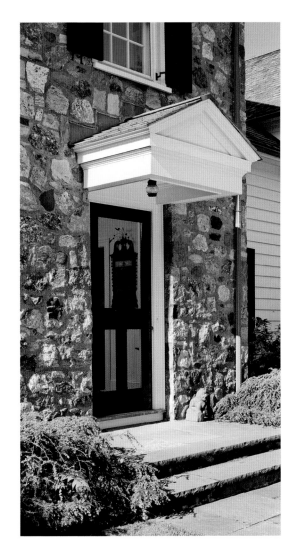

porch, the wall of the house shifts back at a slight angle to allow for steps to come up from the side, as there is no room for them on the sidewalk in front.

Stone House has the simplest kind of projecting entry porch, a gable roof cantilevered without posts or columns, in the manner of Colonial Pennsylvania stone farmhouses. "This choice arose in response to our clients' desire for truly authentic details in their favorite style." Both Farm Cottage and Cape Courtyard House have projecting Classical porticoes with columns and a pediment. In keeping with the overall Colonial Revival feeling of Farm Cottage, the entry porch features paired Tuscan columns and an elliptical arch in the pediment. At Cape Courtyard House, which reinterprets Greek Revival traditions, two Doric columns flank the entrance of the portico, while

the sides are enclosed with shingled walls as windbreaks. Of similar scale, the entry porch at Stable House has a more informal appearance, appropriate to a converted farm structure, with square posts rather than Classical columns and inviting built-in benches on the sides.

As mentioned in the preceding chapter, the entry to Rotunda House is an unusual domed tower on one side of the house. "While the gable front aligns with those of the adjacent houses to keep the space of the street well defined, when you arrive directly in front of the house you discover, set back from the street, the surprise of a domed rotunda, a special feature not found elsewhere in the area. With its open porch half-projecting out from—and half-scooping into—the main volume of the house, the rotunda clearly signals the entrance and draws you into the house."

LEFT The circular entry porch at Rotunda House is half-"scooped out" and half-projecting from the main body of the house. OPPOSITE The living porch of Arc Cottage accommodates multiple seating areas as it sweeps across the entire width of the house.

LIVING PORCHES

Porches can offer the best of both outdoors and indoors—direct access to nature from the comfort of a cushioned wicker chair. For a porch to function as an outdoor living room, it should be able to accommodate seating and, if space allows, dining. The shade of a porch roof is essential to the enjoyment of outdoor summer sitting. But in planning a large porch one has to be careful not to create so much shade that the adjacent interior rooms become shrouded in darkness.

Arc Cottage's porch curves around the facade, offering a variety of vantage points from which to survey the view. The windows in the gable above the porch roof light the upper portion of the double-height living room. Thus, the living room remains filled with light even though the porch roof shades its lower windows.

In Secret Garden House, the architects designed an intimate, sheltered alcove at one end of the waterside porch, complete with a massive stone fireplace and window seat. Sitting around the fire on a cool evening, you can see the water to one side and the garden to the other, dramatically framed by an open, shingled arch. Mountaintop House has two porch pavilions, one an entrance and the other an outdoor living room, which, like Secret Garden House, has a fireplace for evening and cloudy-day coziness. On clear days the porch affords sweeping views of the surrounding countryside.

ABOVE At Mountaintop House the living porch at left and entry porch at right are twin pavilions that reach out from the house to engage with the outdoor living space. OPPOSITE At Secret Garden House a cozy alcove with a fireplace and built-in seat occupies one end of the porch. OVERLEAF The large living porch at Mountaintop House features a fireplace and spacious seating area.

ABOVE Cape Porch House reflects the vernacular Greek Revival character of its neighbors. As seen from the water, the broad porch reinforces the apparent symmetry of the house, though the house is not, in fact, symmetrical. OPPOSITE, LEFT Simple but refined, the massive square posts of Farm Villa impart a monumental quality to its porch. OPPOSITE, RIGHT Rugged tree-trunk columns and "shark's teeth"–cut shingles give the porch of Family Camp a rustic air.

EXTERIORS

At Cape Porch House there are two living porches, one open and the other screened. Nothing says summer living like a screened porch. Situated on the side of the house opposite the water view, this screened porch is for evening use, when the bugs are biting. The expansive open porch facing the water is the main daytime living space. Just one step above the ground, it enables one to glide effortlessly from house to porch to lawn.

In a more whimsical vein, the porch of Family Camp makes playful use of many rustic motifs, including sawtooth-cut shingles and tree-trunk columns complete with bark and branch stubs. Most whimsical of all are the exposed rafter ends, cut and painted to resemble boars' heads (hence the place's nickname, Snout House).

PUBLIC &

In approaching and entering a house one makes a transition, in stages, from public to private. Courtyards and porches help mark the passage from the public realm of the road to the private space of the interior. AR&T reinforce the distinction between public and private in the design of the façades of their houses. Often the façade that addresses the road or driveway is different in character from that facing the garden or view. One strategy they have employed is the use of fewer or smaller windows on the entry side to shield the owners from public view, and more or bigger windows on the garden or view side to open the house to the outdoors without compromising privacy. Harbor Cottage, Stone House, Arc Cottage, Island House, Farm Villa, and Water House all take this approach. At Arc Cottage the high, arched entrance is welcoming, if somewhat formal, whereas the garden side seems lower and more casual, as if in response to the leisurely activity of sitting in the comfortable wicker chairs on the broad porch and contemplating the view. The two sides are further distinguished at Water House and Farm Villa by a shift of style. The entrance façade of Water House, with its bands of small-paned windows, is reminiscent of a 1920s beach club, while the water side is more modern, with expansive sliding glass doors and large, undivided windows. The entry side of Farm Villa has the steeply pitched roof, two-over-two double-hung windows, and additive sheds of Vermont farmhouses, whereas the side overlooking the dramatic mountain landscape adopts the grander, more generous aspect of a Neoclassical villa.

1A Water House driveway side with bands of small windows; 1B water side with large areas of glass.

2A Island House driveway side with an artful arrangement of small windows; 2B water side with large dormers, big windows, and expansive porch.

3A Arc Cottage entry side with few windows and tall arch; 3B garden side with oversize windows and broad, sweeping porch.

4A Farm Villa entry side as a vernacular farmhouse; 4B view side as a Neoclassical villa.

5A Harbor Cottage driveway side with a band of high windows; 5B water side with big-scaled double-hung and bay windows.

6A Stone House driveway side with smaller windows and greater expanse of stone wall; 6B field side with more windows, including two large bays.

PRIVATE

2a

3a

2b

3b

5a

6a

5b

6b

DECKS

Open decks—porches without roofs—are good for sunny outdoor living. Yet at Harbor Cottage, even the open deck has the feeling of a living room, as it is partially enclosed by a low, shingled wall that shields it from the driveway and furnished with built-in benches, comfortable chairs, and even a rug. This design pairs the intimacy of a seating area with expansive views of the marshes and cove. For Keystone Cottage AR&T created a two-part transition from interior to exterior with a covered veranda that leads to an open-air deck. From the living room this sequence carries your eye out to the view.

LEFT Harbor Cottage's deck, overlooking the marsh and harbor beyond, features integral planters and built-in benches. OPPOSITE At Keystone Cottage a covered veranda leads to an open deck. This is part of a visual sequence that extends from the living room to a distant water view.

ARCADES AND COLONNADES

Arcades and colonnades are linear covered porches that can connect separate structures, create a path alongside or toward a building, or form a shallow layer of space between indoors and outdoors. Arcades have arches (loosely defined), whereas colonnades have columns.

At Tower House, the long connector between the house and the garage is a hybrid, with arches (cutouts in a cedar-sided wall) on the water side and columns (simple wood posts) as a continuation of the entry porch facing the driveway.

ABOVE The garage of Tower House is connected to the main structure by a covered colonnade/arcade that helps to separate the arrival area from the water-side outdoor living space. OPPOSITE The entry door at Secret Garden House opens onto a long colonnade that leads the visitor past the garden before gaining access to the actual house.

EXTERIORS
▲

In both Secret Garden House and Cape Courtyard House, the apparent front door opens not directly into the house but into a colonnade that skirts the garden courtyard and leads to the real front door. In each case there is the delightful surprise of discovering the hidden courtyard and an interesting processional sequence through the colonnade to the entrance. "This is all a form of choreography."

At Arcade House, you first enter a "gate lodge" near the road that contains two small garages flanking the entrance. A latticed arcade connects the gate lodge in an axial path through the middle of a garden courtyard to the house itself. The arcade is high, maintaining a continuous roof ridge from the gate lodge to the house. The lattice panels serve as a kind of decorative frieze spanning the distance from the posts supporting them to the roofline. "It's a grand way to enter a small house."

One of the firm's most dramatic uses of this architectural device is the entrance to Harbor Cottage, where a steep-roofed, wooden Gothic arcade extends forty feet out from the house and leads the visitor from the parking area to a massive entrance door ornamented with delicate Gothic muntins. "The arcade is wide enough for two to walk arm-in-arm to the front door." Again, a small house is augmented by a grand ceremonial gesture.

The dramatic arcade at Harbor Cottage is like the house as a whole, inspired by a mix of sources, including at least two favorite summer chapels.

COLUMNS

Columns are one of the basic structural elements of architecture, the vertical posts that hold things up. They can be expressive, showing the heavy weight of the structure they support or, on the contrary, its lightness. The proportions of the column shaft and the details its cap and base are the for this expressiveness and an occasion for endless variation. are also primary style markers. Classical columns are governed by rules developed over the centuries and codified as the Orders. But even the classical orders can be molded to suit the circumstances. Other styles have their own characteristic columns, and a new style can be signaled by a invented of column details.

TOP ROW FROM LEFT Riverview House: Thick, plain Greek Doric columns are sturdy supports for a country porch. Winnepocket House: A single column at the entry is carved from a rustic log. Family Camp: Tree trunks with bark and branches add to the flavor of this cabin on a Maine island. Pasture House: A specially invented order includes brackets holding dangling wooden "eggs," which are attached each Easter and taken down in the winter.

MIDDLE ROW FROM LEFT Arcade House: Square posts support a decorative trellis that spans from the "gate lodge" to the house. Mountaintop House: Shingled porch posts are capped with the zigzag motif that recurs throughout the house. Portico house: The addition of a Greek Doric portico dignifies the entrance to this otherwise plain old house.

BOTTOM ROW FROM LEFT Gable in a Square: Rectangular posts respond to the plane of the wall they support. Six Gables: Posts with brackets help impart a medieval flavor. Island Hill House: Tuscan columns give this porch a temple-like feeling. Arc Cottage: Paired cylindrical columns without entasis are a stylized updating of the traditional form.

INTE

RIORS

ENTRANCE HALLS, STAIRS, AND PASSAGES

JUST AS THE SEQUENCE of exterior spaces leading to the entrance can be orchestrated in an interesting way, the act of getting from here to there inside the house can be celebrated or enlivened. An entrance hall can delight you with an unexpected shape, a dramatic view of the rest of the interior, or a spatially exciting stair. A stair can, through its shape and detailing, express grandeur or simplicity and reveal ever-changing perspectives as you ascend or descend. A hallway or passage can be a lively space in itself, with windows or light from above, alcoves for seating or bookcases, or some variation of ceiling height. "If the main living rooms are places to pause, stairs and passages are places of motion. They are the connective tissue of a house." AR&T have explored a variety of solutions for stairs and passages that give their houses spatial richness and contribute to their flavor.

Passages for horizontal circulation and stairs for vertical circulation establish visual connections and allow you to navigate through the house. A clear pattern of circulation makes it easier to find your way. AR&T often establish axial views through the building to make a small house seem bigger, to set forth pathways of movement, and to bring order to either a formal or informal plan.

PRECEDING PAGES An octagonal hall lit from above is the centerpiece of the interior at Red House. OPPOSITE Stairs and passages are the connective tissue of a house. "The cloister" at Mountaintop House gracefully descends a step at a time while linking all the main rooms.

▲

ENTRANCE HALLS

The entrance hall sets the stage for your first impression of the interior. "From time to time our clients ask for an entrance hall that is bigger than absolutely necessary, even in a small house, to make a welcoming, generous impression." In AR&T's houses the character of the entrance hall sometimes corresponds to expectations set by the exterior but in other cases surprises you or sets you up for a later surprise. "We like the entry to give clear signals, but not necessarily give everything away."

At Harbor Cottage, you pass through a generously wide Dutch door, the glass in its upper

half ornamented with a Gothic pattern of pointed arches. The door is an extension of the exterior Gothic arcade that leads you there, but inside the style shifts to that of a simple summer cottage with high, beaded-board wainscoting and country doors with five horizontal panels. The front door is dark green, like the exterior trim, but the interior doors are a refreshing and unusual purple. The arcade could make the entry dark, but a lantern tower above the door, where the arcade roof meets the main roof, sends light flooding down into the hall. You enter facing a wall: straight ahead is a table, a place to put the mail or a vase of flowers. "The view of the water is blocked, and you are that much more gratified to see it when you turn to enter the living room. It is clear that you are meant to turn left to get to the living room, because its doorway is the widest opening in the entry."

Winnepocket House, too, is entered through a wide, oversize Dutch door with glass in the upper half. The entrance hall is like a broad landing of the stair that spills down from the second floor and continues down two steps to the living room. Stepping down to the living room lends a ceremonious feel to the entrance and causes the room to seem grander. This gesture is tempered, however, by the wide, rough-sawn planks on the walls and by the

OPPOSITE At Harbor Cottage a Gothic-style Dutch door opens into the entry hall, which is lit from above. TOP RIGHT The balusters of the stair at Winnepocket House are flat cutouts in the shape of traditional turned spindles, giving a rural vernacular feeling to the entry hall. BOTTOM RIGHT The two steps marking the transition from the entry to the main living area lend a ceremonious element.

countrified, vernacular treatment of the stair, which has flat wooden cutouts for balusters. "Early American vernacular imagery is combined with a more generously flowing sense of space." The entrance is uncluttered with closets, but a mud room opens directly off it through a wide opening.

At Rocksyde the entrance hall is a rotunda, no hint of which can be gleaned from the quietly shingled exterior. Not only does it wow visitors but its round shape also helps resolve a shift of axis from the front door to the pathway leading back through the house. The walls of the rotunda are of painted wood that is "rusticated" to resemble courses of cut stone. The ceiling's ornamental ribs suggest a dome. The black-and-white color scheme is dramatic and elegant. Using simple means and materials, AR&T have given the impression of something fancier and more monumental. "It's a strategy that has been employed throughout history."

STAIRS

Stairs are among the most complex parts of a house, and they offer some of the greatest opportunities for invention and delight. AR&T sometimes minimize or hide the stair if the second floor contains seldom-used rooms or is meant to be private. But more often they call attention to it and single it out for emphasis. They pay particular attention to the ratio of riser height to tread width, which determines how comfortable it is to climb or descend. "The whole stair doesn't have to be wide to be grand or generous. More important is that it be gradual rather than steep, and have some space around it."

OPPOSITE The entry to Rocksyde is an unexpected rotunda that cleverly shifts the axis of movement from the front door to the rooms beyond.

For AR&T a stair that turns, with one or more landings, is always more appealing and less fatiguing to climb than a straight one. At Riverview House the stair turns four times, and it incorporates a built-in bench. "It draws on the example of great Shingle-style stairs, such as that at H. H. Richardson's Stonehurst, which function not just as a passageway but as an occupiable space." The stair at Riverview House promotes horizontal as well as vertical connections, opening to the dining room through a screen of spindles and thereby adding a layer of spatial richness.

At Cape Tower House the stair follows the shape of its octagonal tower, leaving a generous open space in the center. "The railing, made not of spindles but of boards with cutouts, borrows from a Swedish country house that our clients admired." The band of windows around the upper part of the tower lights not only the stair but also the whole hall below.

The stair at Lake Library snakes around the inside of its round tower. "There is no supporting center post, which would have made construction easier. At the center is an open space around which the continuous railing spirals, uninterrupted by newel posts. Running your hand along that sinuous wooden rail is a pleasant tactile experience." The windows are not organized in a band around the top of the tower, as at Cape Tower House, but are vertical slits that play on the miniature castle imagery.

ABOVE With its multiple landings and built-in bench, the stair at Riverview House functions not only as vertical circulation but also as occupiable space. OPPOSITE At Cape Tower House boards with cutouts form the stair rail in a variation on the more traditional spindle railing.

After it reaches the first landing, the stair at Farm Cottage leaves the security of the perimeter walls and goes leaping through space to the other side of its hall. In traversing the hall from the front door to the garden-facing porch, you pass beneath the stair. The stair hall is lit from above by the same type of dormers that serve all the second-floor rooms. No special window configuration on the exterior draws attention to the stair hall. "The modesty of the exterior gives little hint of this bold, sculptural object seemingly suspended in a soaring space."

At Rocksyde, too, the stair seems to fly through space, as the treads—which look like blocks stacked on a diagonal and are held together with concealed steel—cascade past a huge window. "The stair, open on the other side to the dining room and with no support from below, tries to be as transparent as possible to let the light from the big south-facing window filter through to the room beyond." The stacked, block-like steps derive from any number of Georgian- and Federal-style stairs, but the

ABOVE The stair rail at Lake Library snakes upward in a continuous spiral. Slit windows in the stair tower play on the imagery of castles. OPPOSITE The stair at Farm Cottage dramatically flies across the open space of the central hall.

jazzy, alternating black-and-white color scheme, like the keys of a piano, has a precedent in Edwin Lutyens's Gledstone Hall of 1923.

The wow factor of the stair hall at Cape Courtyard House is the ceiling, a barrel vault of simple wood slats. "The barrel vault calls to mind Romanesque church naves or H. H. Richardson libraries, but the main point of the vault is to bring down the height of the walls surrounding the stair and modulate

the scale of the space." The stair does not end at the second-floor landing but continues to climb right up into the space of the vaulted ceiling, until it reaches a cozy platform with a window seat overlooking the sea. Again, AR&T have made part of the stair a usable living area.

The full height of the stair hall at Six Gables is visually reduced by wrapping the hall in a wainscoting that stops halfway up the walls of the second floor. The painted wainscoting looks like Old World paneling, but it is produced in the simplest way, by applying strips of wood in a grid over plywood. "Care and expense were reserved for the newel post, which is carved to conform with the medieval flavor of other decorative elements throughout the house."

The quick-and-easy method of paneling around the stair was also used at Checkerboard House. In this case, the strips of wood are applied not even to plywood but to sheetrock. "This small area of paneling organizes what would have been an awkwardly shaped, left-over bit of wall next to the stair and makes the

OPPOSITE The stair at Cape Courtyard House rises through the barrel-vaulted entry hall and culminates on the upper landing in a broad window seat facing the ocean. ABOVE Supported by concealed steel plates, the distinctive black-and-white "piano key" stair of Rocksyde also flies through open space.

stair of an otherwise very simply detailed house more special." At Keystone Cottage, too, AR&T used very simple means to set the stair apart as a special object. It is wrapped in a half-wall, or parapet, of painted beaded board that contrasts in texture with the smooth, plastered walls of the hall. Here again, as in many of AR&T's stair halls, the high space is used to bring light from above into the middle of the house.

LEFT At Checkerboard House a "shortcut" paneling of strips of wood applied to sheetrock organizes the irregular wall next to the stair. RIGHT A parapet of beaded board that contrasts with the smooth texture of the interior walls lends distinction to the stair at Keystone Cottage. OPPOSITE Wood banding over plywood creates the effect of Old World paneling in the stair hall of Six Gables.

INTERIORS

▲

122

PASSAGES

A hallway can be much more than a mere connector of rooms. Architectural features can enhance the experience of moving through a house. At Mountaintop House a distinctive passage that AR&T call "the cloister" serves as the entrance hall and also connects all the main rooms of the first floor. It descends from the main entrance in gradual steps that follow the slope of the site. You move axially from one end of the cloister to the other and also across it from the dining room to French doors that open onto the garden. The cloister is flooded with sunlight from its south-facing windows, which march along in a regular rhythm. Unlike the rest of the interior, the walls of the cloister are covered with cedar shingles, which impart a semi-outdoor character and give a nod of reference to the shingled interior of a favorite nearby summer chapel. "We're always fascinated with the in-between zones, the layer of space between inside and outside."

On the second floor of Mountaintop House a passage connects the bathrooms, dressing rooms, and bedroom of the master suite. A series of incidents along the way keeps it interesting. On the right an oriel—a nook

LEFT The second-floor hall in Mountaintop House is enhanced by a window seat set in an oriel that projects from the house to capture a distant view. OPPOSITE The interior walls of "the cloister" at Mountaintop House are shingled, imparting an outdoor feeling to the passageway.

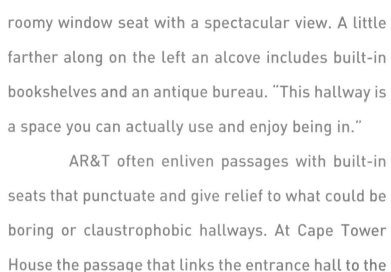

that hangs off the outside of the house—contains a roomy window seat with a spectacular view. A little farther along on the left an alcove includes built-in bookshelves and an antique bureau. "This hallway is a space you can actually use and enjoy being in."

AR&T often enliven passages with built-in seats that punctuate and give relief to what could be boring or claustrophobic hallways. At Cape Tower House the passage that links the entrance hall to the back door has a bench in an alcove next to the coat closet where you can sit down to take off your boots. A glossy white wainscoting keeps it cheerful.

Mews House and Long House both feature long axial passages that lead you straight from the front door all the way through the house. The entrances of both houses are on the narrow end fac-

ABOVE A built-in seat in the hallway at Cape Tower House expands the sense of space and offers a convenient perch to take off your boots. FAR LEFT AND LEFT At Mews House an alignment of openings leads you in an axial path straight from the front door to the living room. OPPOSITE, LEFT At Long House an axial route takes you past some rooms and through others. OPPOSITE, RIGHT At Farm Cottage axial views connect the main rooms.

ing the street, and the strong through-axis makes it clear how to get to the main rooms. At Mews

House there is a straight shot from the front door, through the entrance hall, through another hall,

through the dining room, and finally to the living room, with a window at the end of the axis. "There's

no doubt which way you're meant to go, even though the living room is far from the entrance. And you

have a varied set of experiences along the way."

AR&T created long axial views and paths of movement at Farm Cottage as well, but not with

hallways; instead, they aligned doorways and windows to let you see and move from room to room

through the whole house. "You enjoy the expansiveness of the long vistas combined with the rich-

ness of looking through many layers. It's a configuration known as an enfilade, or line, of rooms, borrowed from grand houses of the past." In renovating Stable House, AR&T reorganized a jumbled existing plan and aligned openings to reveal a vista that not only connects the kitchen to the dining room but also passes through a pantry and entry hall. The kitchen now seems closer to the dining room, even though it isn't, and it is easier to navigate between the two.

At Red House a grand circulation hall lit by a rooftop cupola occupies the very heart of the house. The octagonal space is defined on the lower level by substantial Doric columns, calling to mind the columnar halls of Palladian villas or the atriums of Roman houses. A balcony on the second floor encircles and overlooks the lower hall. Standing in the entry vestibule you see straight through

the octagonal room to the stair, which spills toward you in concentric circles, and through an interior window behind the stair to the dining room. "There is an axial view, but your movement along that axis is blocked, and you have to skirt the stair to move through the house. In a private house paths of circulation don't always have to be obvious, and playfully confounding your sense of direction introduces a sense of mystery."

OPPOSITE In the renovation of Stable House the architects reorganized the plan to open up visual connections between the rooms. ABOVE At Red House the octagonal hall draws you in and at the same time playfully diverts your path of movement.

ENTRANCE HALLS, STAIRS, AND PASSAGES

INTERIOR

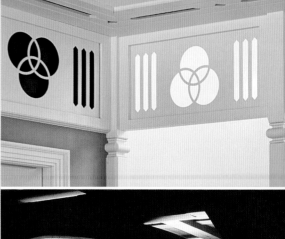

Interior details have many jobs to do. In the realm of construction, moldings cover joints; newel posts anchor stair rails in place; brackets support shelves. From a functional point of view, shelves hold books or other objects; railings keep you from falling; screens of spindles or other elements define spaces without completely enclosing them. And on the level of meaning or pure aesthetic delight, boards with cut-out shapes can convey a favorite image of the owners; a pattern of battens on a ceiling organizes and embellishes an oddly shaped or drab surface; an arch above a door lends importance and elegance to an otherwise plain opening.

AR&T design interior details with all of these purposes in mind. They also use details to set the tone or style of their interiors. Their rustic, urbane, and modern interiors are defined not only by materials but also by details. The Colonial Revival character of Stone House, for example, is established by the molded casings, the crown moldings, and such details as the fan arches over the living room doorways. Mountaintop House derives its rustic camp feeling from a consistent language of details based on the zigzag motif. As often as not AR&T's details, such as the ribbed dome of the entrance rotunda at Rocksyde or the interior post capitals at Cypress House, transcend historical precedents and imbue their interiors with visual richness in a fresh way.

TOP ROW FROM LEFT
Rocksyde: The dining room frieze becomes a screen across the stair. A pattern of battens on the library ceiling gives an order to the irregular shape. Wood ribs suggest a dome in the entry rotunda.

MIDDLE ROW FROM LEFT
Six Gables: Violin cutouts ornament the railing of the "musicians' gallery." Long House: Brackets support a high shelf for books and objects. Mountaintop House: Vertical slats screen the stair from the entry hall. Stone House: Fan details give more importance to the living room doorways.

BOTTOM ROW FROM LEFT
Six Gables: The carved newel post is inspired by medieval paneling. Farm Cottage: A mirrored Palladian "window" surmounts the mantel. Cypress House: A new order makes its appearance. Checkerboard House: Simple paneling organizes the stair wall.

DETAILS

LIVING ROOMS, LIBRARIES, AND DINING ROOMS

IN RECENT DECADES, interior arrangements have grown increasingly informal, though the degree of informality remains a matter of individual taste. Functions that were once kept separate are now often combined. Many people are willing to dispense with a separate dining room, for example, and put tables for dining either in the living room or the kitchen, or both. Open plans are ever more popular; the expanded visual connections between rooms allow even small houses to seem spacious. AR&T's approach is usually to maintain the sense that a room has a distinct shape, even if there are large openings between rooms.

Houses with open plans, accommodating the informality as well as the equipment of modern living, can still have the flavor that people find appealing in architecture of the past. In AR&T's interiors, historical references are there, certainly, yet the rooms are decidedly "modern" in their use. Their interiors tend to maintain a thematic and stylistic relationship to the exterior, creating a consistency of design throughout the structure. But AR&T are not dogmatic about the correspondence between the interior and the exterior. Interiors and exteriors have their own requirements,

OPPOSITE One lofty room at Lake Library combines several functions:
living room, dining room, library, and small hidden kitchenette.

which may sometimes diverge. "Whereas some find a virtue in being able to 'read' the interior from outside, we are more apt to try for some element of surprise, not revealing on the exterior everything about the interior."

Most of AR&T's living spaces can be grouped stylistically into three categories: rustic, urbane, and modern. "There's a place for all three of these points on the spectrum, and some of our clients are lucky enough to have more than one. Within each of us, there are leanings toward one way of living, but times when we're more inclined toward another." The rustic interiors are usually for vacation or country houses and often feature wood with a natural finish. The urbane interiors may be for town or country houses; they may incorporate some Classical details and compositional devices; and they are usually painted. Classical interior details in some form appear equally in houses with Shingle-style, Greek Revival, or Colonial Revival tendencies. The modern interiors are clean and simple, without many moldings. They depend on pleasing proportions and quality of light, without the help of the flavor and associations evoked by references to past styles. These categories are not absolute and sometimes blur one into the other.

RUSTIC INTERIORS

A cabin with exposed studs and rafters, Family Camp represents the far end of the rustic scale. The interior finish is the same as the exterior wall and roof sheathing—unpainted boards. As a summer retreat on a Maine island, Family Camp gives its occupants a bracingly refreshing change of scene from their life in the city. Living, dining, and sleeping all take place in one big room. "The cabin is the ultimate expression of the simple life, but the effect can be achieved only with care. The proportions of the space and of the window openings have to be calculated as thoroughly as in a more finished house, and the placement of each stud and electrical device must be well thought out, as they are all exposed."

The "camp" theme carries through Fishing Cabin as well. The design is meant to evoke the character of some of the almost shack-like old fishing clubhouses that still stand along the stream. More than half of its interior is a lodge hall, extending to the full height of the roof and centered on a stone fireplace massive enough to walk into. This room, encompassing living and dining, is surprisingly

OPPOSITE An informal room at SeaBend combines living and dining and is open to the kitchen beyond.
LEFT With exposed studs and rafters, the interior of Family Camp is perhaps AR&T's most rustic.

grand, belying the modest appearance of the exterior. It is more finished than Family Camp, "pan-eled with fir beaded board stained in a mellow tone that will improve with age and exposure to the owner's cigar smoke."

Lake Library, a new guesthouse for an old summer house on a lake in the White Mountains of New Hampshire, also contains a lodge-like living space that occupies more than half the volume of the building. "The room is rustic, cozy, and grand at the same time." The height of the space and the upward sweep of the enormous, vertical bay window impart grandeur, but it is tempered by the warmth of the unfinished pine paneling and the rusticity of the trim details, which are cut in the angular

manner of Adirondack camp detailing. The massive stone fireplace is a major focal point. Despite all the wood and stone, the room, which incorporates a dining table, a library, and a kitchen concealed in a cabinet, is flooded with light from the south-facing bay window and the rooftop light monitor.

Perhaps the grandest of AR&T's wood-clad living rooms is that of Six Gables, with its massive wooden trusses made of lumber reclaimed from old mill buildings. It has the feeling of a baronial hall but remains intimate thanks in part to the low, human-scale side walls. The balcony, with its railing of violin-shaped cutouts, overlooks the room from one end and recalls in a modest, lighthearted way the musicians' galleries of old castles. And, in fact, "the children do practice the violin there."

OPPOSITE Fishing Cabin plays upon the rustic theme with stained wood paneling and a massive stone fireplace. ABOVE LEFT AND RIGHT Lake Library also features wood-paneled walls and a large stone fireplace. A soaring bay window fills the room with light. OVERLEAF, LEFT AND RIGHT At Six Gables, in the grandest of AR&T's wood interiors, the balcony, with its violin-shaped cutouts, recalls the musicians' galleries of medieval castles. Huge trusses milled from reclaimed timbers support the roof.

Mountaintop House also envelops you in the warm glow of oiled wood. "The first-floor interiors are all wood, like the interior of a rustic camp. The decorative theme is developed through wood details such as the frieze of crisscross boards around the living room and dining room, and other zigzag details on mantels, cabinets, and newel posts. This language of detailing represents the kind of work a carpenter in the backwoods could execute, but the result is visually rich." As Mountaintop House steps down the hill, one room flows into the next and the ceiling height of each successive room increases. "East to west, the sequence progresses from a low, intimate library to a higher kitchen and dining room to a yet higher living room."

ABOVE AND OPPOSITE The oiled-wood interior gives Mountaintop House a rustic camp aura. The crisscross and sawtooth ornamentation is simple yet visually rich.

URBANE INTERIORS

Cape Tower House has two living rooms, one at each end of the house, identical in size and layout but entirely different in character. The living room next to the dining room is painted white; the other, next to the kitchen, where the family reads or watches TV, is wood-paneled. Both rooms have moldings and mantels in the Colonial Revival tradition, but it's remarkable what a different feeling their materials and colors give them. "Even within a given style, there are nearly infinite possibilities for varying the feeling and ambience of a room as appropriate to its use."

In the living room of Cape Courtyard House the high, white wainscoting helps keep the scale intimate. The massive square posts flanking the entry and the broad, flat door casings are in the simplified vernacular Greek Revival consistent with the rest of the house. The focus of the room is on

At Cape Tower House two similar living rooms are
very different in feeling. OPPOSITE One is lined with naturally
finished wood for a warm, library-like atmosphere.
ABOVE The other, at the opposite end of the house, is painted white.

the fireplace, and because it is located on one of the short end walls of the long, rectangular room, two seating areas are possible. The fireplace at Secret Garden House is also positioned at one end of the living room, which accommodates not only two seating areas but also the dining table. With floor-to-ceiling bookcases, the whole room takes on the character of a library. "Our client is a writer who loves to be surrounded by books."

On a cozier scale, the Rotunda House living room also doubles as a library, with a floor-to-ceiling wall of books. "There's nothing like books to make a room seem lived in and to express the personality and interests of the inhabitants. And visually, the books add color and texture to the room." At Rocksyde, a Classically detailed opening in a wall of books leads to an inviting alcove with window seat. "The bookcases make the wall thick, and that extra thickness enhances the experience of passing through to the alcove."

ABOVE At Rocksyde a classically detailed portal leads through a wall of books to a small alcove off the living room. OPPOSITE, TOP The main living and dining space at Secret Garden House is also a library. OPPOSITE, BOTTOM A wall of books also enriches the living room of Rotunda House. OVERLEAF A high white wainscoting gives the living room of Cape Courtyard House a summery feeling.

MODERN INTERIORS

The exterior of Cape Porch House is rendered in a vernacular Greek Revival manner to harmonize with its neighbors. But for their living spaces, "the owners wanted something entirely different, a serene, minimalist, white world." The rooms provide a neutral background for an eclectic collection of antique and modern furniture. Everything is pared down to essentials, without moldings or varied textures. In a plan geared to informal summer living, the stairs occupy one side of the living room and are set apart only by a plain, white, plastered parapet wall rather than a more detailed railing. Similarly, the interior of Farm Villa is a minimalist set of spaces inside a house that, on the exterior, is a cross between a Vermont farmhouse and a Neoclassical villa. "The outside connects the house to traditions both of the place and of the family, and the inside represents a fresh way of living."

LEFT In contrast to its exterior—part Vermont farmhouse, part Neoclassical villa—a modern spirit infuses the interiors of Farm Villa. OPPOSITE At Cape Porch House the unornamented white interiors allow the owners' collection of antique and modern furniture to stand out.

DINING ROOMS

Dining rooms, though less common than in the past, are still alive and well. "A separate dining room can give you more scope for orchestrating a dinner party, putting the focus on the table, and controlling the lighting." The dining room of Cape Porch House, in keeping with the modern orientation of its interiors, has white walls without moldings. Because the large family frequently gathers for meals in this room, it occupies the center of the house, opening onto the kitchen, the living room, the library, and the screened porch.

AR&T sometimes let the dining room do double duty as a passage to the living room or the kitchen, avoiding unnecessary hallways. "Unlike living rooms, dining rooms can be walk-through

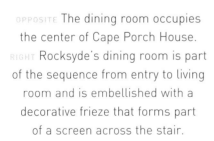

OPPOSITE The dining room occupies the center of Cape Porch House.
RIGHT Rocksyde's dining room is part of the sequence from entry to living room and is embellished with a decorative frieze that forms part of a screen across the stair.

spaces without suffering from the traffic." At Rocksyde the dining room is part of the pathway from

the entrance to the living room and is also open to the striking main stair. The stair is screened from

the dining room by a colonnade and a frieze of Japanesque motifs that continues around the room.

"The frieze helps give the space definition and character and also lowers the scale of the walls in a

room that is meant for sitting."

The dining rooms of Mountaintop House and Farm Cottage, in their different ways, take

the opportunity to include built-in sideboards in alcoves. The cabinets hold table linens and uten-

ABOVE The dining room at Farm Cottage is made special
by a deep coved ceiling. OPPOSITE At Family Camp a
vernacular version of a rose window presides over
the whimsical pencil-leg "drawing room" table.

sils and provide a surface for serving. The alcoves also are places for hanging pictures and placing sconces that help light the room. At Mountaintop House the sideboard alcove doubles as a partial room divider between the dining and living rooms.

The "Drawing Room" at the rustic-themed Family Camp is a pavilion that functions as a projects and game room for the whole extended family but can also house the annual summer banquet for twenty. The table legs are whimsically shaped like pencils, for "drawing." "Dining rooms, which may seem like an extravagance, can actually be flexible and adaptable to multiple uses."

ABOVE AND OPPOSITE At Mountaintop House a
built-in sideboard occupies an alcove that partially
screens the dining room from the living room.

FIREPLACES

The focal point of many rooms is the fireplace and its mantel. In fact, *focus* is the Latin word for "fireplace." Fireplaces today provide atmosphere, "warming the soul" rather than heating the house. We still instinctively want to gather around the hearth, clustering our seating there. In keeping with AR&T's belief in emphasis, the fireplace is often the element of the room that receives the most attention and ornament. The mantel is where AR&T has the most fun, devising spirited interpretations of familiar precedents.

AR&T's fireplaces range from rugged stone to delicately detailed painted wood, in keeping with the spirit of the room. The surround that occupies the space between the wood mantel and the firebox itself can be stone, brick, or tile. Some clients like tile with decorations that have a special meaning to them. Some like a raised hearth, which puts the fire closer to eye level, and others prefer a more traditional hearth flush with the floor, which allows you to pull your chair up close. Sometimes the fireplace is part of an intimately scaled alcove or inglenook and incorporates built-in seating.

When a room has both a fireplace and a TV, the trick is always to devise an arrangement that allows you to look at both. One solution, made possible by flat-screen TVs, is to conceal a TV in a panel above the fireplace.

TOP ROW FROM LEFT:
SeaBend: Angular Arts and Crafts–style mantel brackets relate to the owners' furnishings. Cape Tower House: Stock moldings are combined in an elegant mantel. Six Gables: A massive stone fireplace warms the screened porch in the evening. The living room mantel, which shares the same chimney, is designed around a portrait.

MIDDLE ROW FROM LEFT
Long House: The mantel wraps around the chimney breast. Harbor Cottage: A pillow-like molding supports the mantel shelf.

BOTTOM ROW FROM LEFT
Mountaintop House: Zigzag brackets and moldings relate the library mantel to the overall decorative theme. Farmyard House: A built-in bench provides a perch next to the fire. Winnepocket House: Scalloped brackets support the mantel shelf. Rotunda House: The fireplace surround is a big-scaled bracket.

KITCHENS, BATHROOMS, AND BEDROOMS

KITCHENS

OVER THE CENTURIES, no room has undergone greater transformation than the kitchen. In Colonial America, the kitchen centered around an enormous brick hearth; it was a multipurpose room, often incorporating cooking, eating, socializing, even sleeping. Over time, kitchens in simpler houses maintained this mix of functions, whereas bigger houses began to include kitchens devoted exclusively to food preparation, usually staffed with servants. These kitchens were kept well out of sight of the main living areas. With the gradual disappearance of servants in the twentieth century, we've come full circle to the kitchen as a social gathering place. Now that the family cooks its own meals, no one wants to be left out of the action, and today's kitchens routinely include an eating area, a sitting area, a TV, a computer, and a place for children to do their homework or for parents to pay the bills.

OPPOSITE The kitchen at Rocksyde is dressed up enough
to serve as part of the path to the living room.

People entertain guests in their kitchens, too, and cooking is part of the evening's diversion. As a result of this shift of use, a space that was not long ago considered wholly utilitarian has evolved into a showplace. "Over the course of our practice kitchens have gotten fancier, with plain, laminate cabinets and ordinary appliances giving way to paneled, furniture-like wood cabinets and professional-looking appliances." The kitchen has become the most prominent room of many households, and indeed, the amount of design and money spent on it now exceeds that of any other area in the house.

Designers who seek to connect with older traditions of architecture don't necessarily want to re-create truly authentic old kitchens, which would seem Spartan, ill-equipped, and poorly located by today's standards. The challenge for AR&T is to create kitchens that are in keeping with the spirit of the rest of the house while incorporating the required functions of contemporary cooking, socializing, and consumption. "It's not that hard to do, as cabinetry in the style of the house works perfectly well for the kitchen. And there are plenty of materials for countertops, backsplashes, and floors that are both practical and handsome."

The modern centrality of the kitchen is clearly acknowledged at Six Gables, where it is a kind of pavilion in the middle of a large room that includes the dining area at one end and a family sitting area at the other. The food-preparation area—a room within a room, defined by massive posts and beams similar to those in the living room—remains open to the living spaces around it. The whole family and their guests can be involved in preparing the meal, and the "chef" is not isolated. At the same time, in style and materials, the design of the kitchen is like that of the rest of the house.

OPPOSITE, TOP The kitchen at Six Gables is a pavilion in the center
of an informal room that also includes dining and sitting areas.
OPPOSITE, BOTTOM LEFT The Cape Tower House kitchen includes a
seating area in the bay window and a table for family dining.
OPPOSITE, BOTTOM RIGHT At Stone House the kitchen is part
of the library/sitting room at the heart of the house.

LML 09

At Cape Tower House cooking, eating, and sitting are all clustered in a fairly compact room. While cooking is in progress, you can sit in a wicker chair in the bay window, and even watch a small TV housed in the central island. The flavor is Colonial Revival, in keeping with the style of the rest of the house. "But there was never a Colonial or Colonial Revival kitchen like this!" The kitchen at Stone House is in a similar style. In this case the table is in the bay window; a sitting area lined with bookshelves is centered on a fireplace with an antique mantel; and the actual kitchen area is almost an incidental appendage to the room, which the owners call the "library."

ABOVE At Riverview House the ceiling of the eating area off of the kitchen is a Sheraton fan motif dramatically enlarged in scale so that it gives the impression of a tent. OPPOSITE The food preparation area is a stylized reinterpretation of early-twentieth-century kitchens, with the addition of whimsical details like the rolling pin refrigerator door handle.

INTERIORS

▲

Perhaps AR&T's boldest kitchen design is the one in Riverview House. The eating area is open to the workspace and to the family sitting area but is defined by an oval ceiling structure that can be read as both a stretched tent and a gigantic rendering of a Sheraton fan motif. "In a nineteenth-century room this motif would appear as a smaller plaster medallion in the middle of the ceiling, but here the center is a void, an oculus that opens to a mysterious space above." The oval breakfast area is half-embedded within the mass of the house and half projecting from it, with a sweeping band of oversize windows that look out on the river and flood the room with natural light. The boldly checked linoleum floor and the chairs, each painted a different color, contribute to the sense of whimsy, which also animates the preparation area—a reinterpretation of the kitchens of the 1920s and 1930s. The soft but playful colors and faux bun feet of the cabinets conjure up these kitchens. The refrigerator lurking behind the V-groove-paneled cabinetry is opened with an elongated rolling-pin handle.

Mountaintop House adapts its camp imagery to a modern, functional kitchen. "The island top is made of reclaimed barn boards, mellow with the patina of age, which our client had the fun of tracking down." The feet of the island and profile of the shelf brackets continue the zigzag motif used throughout the house. The island is painted a different color from the rest of the room to make it seem more like the freestanding furniture of an old kitchen than part of the built-in cabinetry of a modern one. The open shelving is an inexpensive solution reminiscent of old summer camps. "Weekend guests can find what they're looking for in plain view." The more-than-ample lighting comes from old-fashioned schoolhouse fixtures that add to the flavor.

When the occasion calls for it, AR&T also produce sleeker kitchens. In keeping with the modern interiors of Cape Porch House and Farm Villa, their kitchens are white and uncluttered. At Cape Porch House, interior designer Judith Swartwood's bold green-and-white-striped backsplash enlivens the otherwise minimalist design and helps tie the whole kitchen together. At Farm Villa the kitchen fittings form a quiet background that doesn't compete for attention with the view. Natural wood floors, carried through the kitchen from the adjacent spaces, add warmth to the white interior.

LEFT The kitchen at Mountaintop House shares the rustic
ambience of the rest of the interior but accommodates
all the modern necessities and conveniences.

KITCHENS, BATHROOMS, AND BEDROOMS

LEFT AND ABOVE Cape Porch House (above) and Farm Villa
(left) both have sleek, white kitchens in keeping with
the overall minimalist orientation of the interiors.

BATHROOMS

Along with the kitchen, the lowly bathroom has evolved from perfunctory to something approaching glamorous. "The ante has been upped for bathrooms, too, in recent years." Here again, AR&T have adapted historical motifs to modern standards.

At Cape Courtyard House his-and-hers sinks—one on either side of a mirrored partition— are like freestanding furniture that also serves as a room divider. At Cape Tower House beaded-board wainscoting wraps around the bathtub and visually ties the room together. At the other end of the spectrum, Family Camp has an outhouse with a composting toilet and an old claw-foot tub that is filled with a garden hose. The facilities may be somewhat primitive, but the high, tower-like space is a delight.

OPPOSITE At Cape Courtyard House the master bathroom is a large, ocean-facing room in which the fixtures are like freestanding furniture. RIGHT Cape Tower House also features a bathtub with a view.

KITCHENS, BATHROOMS, AND BEDROOMS

OPPOSITE The outhouse that serves the guest quarters at Family Camp revels in its primitive charms: an old claw-foot tub filled by a garden hose, with supplementary hot water provided by a kettle on a Coleman hotplate. ABOVE A ladder allows you to reach and open the transoms for natural ventilation in the tiny but soaring space.

KITCHENS, BATHROOMS, AND BEDROOMS

▲

BEDROOMS

The bedroom is the most private part of the house, the place where we rest and reflect with minimal disturbance, we hope, from others. People have different preferences as to whether the bedroom belongs on the first or second floor. "Bedrooms on the first floor suit those who don't want to climb stairs or who like the possibility of direct access to the outdoors. But others feel secure only if their bedroom is on the second floor. Regardless of which floor it is on, though, the bedroom should be separated as much as possible from the hustle and bustle of daily life in the main living areas. AR&T try, whenever viable, to situate bedrooms for the owners, for children, and for guests in their own separate zones for greater privacy.

When it is desirable for reasons of exterior appearance to keep the eave line of a house low, second-floor bedrooms may occupy the space within the roof and be lit by dormer windows. In fact, the word dormer comes from the French *dormir,* which means "to sleep." The slope of the roof and the intersections of dormers can give rise to bedrooms that are full of quirky angles. But that is part of their charm.

The master bedroom of the gambrel-roofed Cape Tower House has a sloping ceiling and dormers, but it isn't dark or claustrophobic in the least. The main dormer is big enough to accommodate a bank of windows with a panoramic view of the water. In addition, the angles of the wall

---

OPPOSITE, TOP At Stable House a quirky bedroom was created out of an unfinished attic. OPPOSITE, BOTTOM Though tucked within a gambrel roof, the master bedroom at Cape Tower House is a generous space with panoramic views.

and ceiling planes reflect the light and scatter it. Built-in window seats occupy nooks between the roof slope and the chimney.

A cozy bedroom is tucked under the roof of Lake Library. "The second-floor bedroom has low eaves and a band of small windows wrapping around two sides, and you feel as though you're in a tree house." As this room is the only space on the second floor, it was felt that a door was unnecessary. Instead, a screen of turned colonnettes separates the stair from the bedroom.

In other instances, a second-floor bedroom—or a first-floor bedroom in a one-story house— may have an unusually high ceiling. The master bedroom of Mountaintop House features a tray ceiling, borrowing some of the attic space, to gain more height and shape the space in a contained and centered way. Sloping up on all four sides to a flat center, the tray ceiling is like a simplified dome, reinforcing the importance of the master bedroom, the only room on the second floor with such a ceiling.

ABOVE LEFT The small bedroom at the top of the spiral stairs at Lake Library has a treehouse-like feeling. ABOVE RIGHT The exotic headboard in the tower guest room at Harbor Cottage resembles the portal of an Egyptian temple. OPPOSITE At Mountaintop House the master bedroom is distinguished by its tray ceiling with battens.

INTERIORS

The bedroom in the guest tower at Harbor Cottage is a lofty and playful chamber with a built-in headboard in the form of an Egyptian temple portal. The pylons are capped with a flared cornice ornamented with lotuses. In keeping with the Egyptian Revival palette, turquoise stripes augment the steeply pitched ceiling, creating a tent-like effect.

In the master bedroom at Long House a wall of shelves filled with books, ceramics, and other objects makes a dramatic backdrop for the bed. The bottom edge of the shelves steps up and down around the bed, framing it in a kind of ziggurat shape that serves as a headboard.

A wall of books and objects makes a grand backdrop for the bed at Long House. A band of windows, some of which are actually mirrors, wraps around the room high above head height to throw more light.

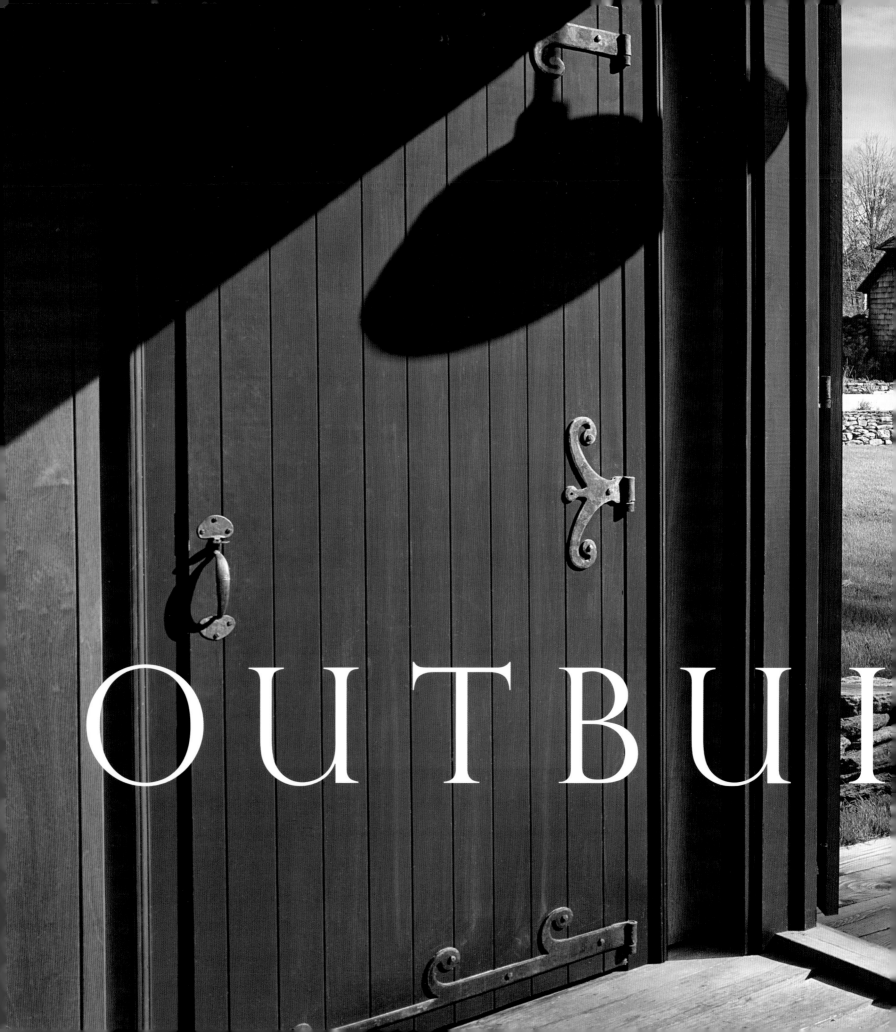

OUTBUI

LDINGS

GUESTHOUSES, BARNS, AND POOL HOUSES

Many of AR&T's houses have one or more secondary structures that augment or reinforce the architectural concepts of the primary building. Grouped together under the term outbuilding, they range from garages and barns to pool houses and guesthouses, and also include studios, children's playhouses, pergolas, and garden sheds. Their intended functions are sometimes combined, as in garages with guest bedrooms above.

The entire complex—the main house and its outbuildings—adds up to more than the sum of its parts. The secondary structures house functions that supplement those of the main house, but AR&T use them as well to define outdoor spaces, to orchestrate the approach to the house, or to frame a view. Outbuildings give the sense of a compound: "They expand the reach of the house and can lend the property a feeling of greater extent."

Stylistically, these structures often match or coordinate with the exterior architecture of the main house, but in some cases they are in deliberate contrast. The Cape Tower House garage is an example of an outbuilding that matches the style and detailing of the main house. Moreover,

---

PRECEDING PAGES The barn at Farmyard House defines one corner of a courtyard. OPPOSITE The barn/studio at Riverview House has an artfully composed façade of asymmetrical but balanced vernacular elements that harmonize with the somewhat higher-style language of parts of the main house.

▲

it serves to complete the entry courtyard by mirroring the guest bedroom wing across from it. The Riverview House barn/studio and Farmyard House barn are slightly toned-down, lower-style versions of the architecture of their respective houses. The Stone House barn does not exactly correspond to the main house but remains within the tradition of vernacular rural structures that would normally accompany a country house. Katonah Pool House, a Carpenter Gothic folly, is a special

retreat at some distance from the main house and a complete departure from it stylistically. "The style of the outbuilding depends partly on its function and partly on its proximity to the main house. But more than the house itself, an outbuilding can be a flight of fancy."

The pool pavilion at Riverview House takes a different tack from the barn/studio, embracing the frivolity of a recreational structure.

GUESTHOUSES, BARNS, AND POOL HOUSES

GUESTHOUSES

Separate guesthouses allow greater privacy for both guests and hosts. "Round-the-clock together-ness isn't always the greatest treat for either." Some of AR&T's guesthouses, where zoning codes and budgets permit, are small, self-contained houses with their own living room and kitchen, while others have only bedrooms and bathrooms. The guesthouse at Mountaintop House is a complete two-bedroom house that defines one side of the arrival courtyard and matches the style of the main house. "It was built first, with the construction of the main house following close behind, and in fact functioned as a sort of laboratory for testing the details that would be used in the larger house."

Lake Library is a complete miniature one-bedroom house that serves as a retreat and library for either the owners or their guests and provides an ideal vantage point for watching tennis matches on the adjacent court. Its materials and colors relate to the hundred-year-old main house, but the flavor is more whimsical. Whereas the main house sprawls across a lawn toward the lake-

ABOVE LEFT AND RIGHT The guesthouse at Mountaintop House
presents a private face to the entry court but opens up to the view
with its own porch. OPPOSITE The starting point for the design of
Lake Library was as a pavilion for watching tennis matches.

front, Lake Library stands up vertically against a backdrop of tall pines. The guesthouse at Harbor Cottage, a tower containing two bedrooms and a bathroom, is also a vertical foil to the more horizontal main house. The main house has a strong, low eave line with exaggerated overhangs, while the guesthouse emphasizes its verticality with board-and-batten siding. "If the house brings to mind one of H. H. Richardson's train stations, the guesthouse is like a railroad watchtower."

At Pasture House the guest wing is connected to the main house by an enclosed passage, but it looks like a separate pavilion with a steep hipped roof, topped by a cupola. "The cupola sweeps up from the roof in a continuous curve like the ventilator of a Shingle-style carriage house." The carriage-house analogy applies to Lantern Gate Lodge as well. The façade overlooking the parking area appears to have a pair of broad, arched carriage doors, but in fact these doors mask a blank wall that preserves the privacy of the guest quarters. "Flanking the false doors are two high little dormers that glow like lanterns or beacons, lighting your approach in the evening."

Several of AR&T's guesthouses are combined with actual garages. Secret Garden House has a square two-car garage with a two-bedroom suite above, surmounted by a pinwheeling hipped roof. "As you move around the building you see that each façade, though asymmetrical, is the same." A similar geometric game, pursued to even more curious effect, is at work at Pinwheel House. "The program is equally unconventional in that this garage for winter storage of a pickup truck serves in summer as the liv-

OPPOSITE Harbor Cottage's guesthouse serves as a vertical foil to the horizontal, one-story main building. ABOVE Lantern Gate Lodge forms a backdrop to the driveway approach. It pretends to be a carriage house but some visitors discover that it is actually a guesthouse.

GUESTHOUSES, BARNS, AND POOL HOUSES

ing room of this rustic guesthouse." The garage doors are oversize French doors that open out to a water view. On the same Maine island, Family Camp also boasts a quirky garage-cum-guesthouse. With dynamic asymmetry, a tiny window hugs one corner of the façade, while in the other corner a surprisingly big window occupies a dormer that seems to pivot like a flap from the roof. "The imaginary conceit is that at summer's end the garage doors open, letting out the air, and the dormer retracts into the roof." These small outbuildings are rich territory for architectural experimentation. In a carefully controlled way, AR&T try to achieve some of the startling juxtapositions of vernacular architecture.

ABOVE Family Camp's guesthouse also serves as a garage. With a studied asymmetry, an oversized window interrupts the roofline. OPPOSITE In its summer guesthouse mode, the French doors of Pinwheel House are thrown open to the view and plastic mooring balls dangle from the points of the jester's-hat roof. In winter the mooring balls are detached, and a truck occupies the guesthouse living room.

BARNS AND GARAGES

AR&T have designed barns for traditional functions, such as the housing of livestock at Stone House or the storing of tractors at Farmyard House. Characteristic barn features are the red board-and-batten siding and stone foundation at Stone House and sliding barn doors topped by horizontal barn lights at Farmyard House. The architects often endow their garages with the character of barns by including elements such as second-story hayloft doors, as at Stable House, complete with a pulley for hoisting heavy loads to the attic. The garage doors themselves are modern overhead doors that rise with the touch of a button, but they are detailed to look like old swinging barn doors with X-bracing. At Mountaintop House the hayloft door in the attic of the garage has morphed into a tall window that begins to suggest a studio. "We look for ways to take the curse of suburbia off the garage and channel its imagery in more romantic or rural directions."

ABOVE AND OPPOSITE Garages at Stable House (above left) and Mountaintop House (above right) take on the character of barns like that at Stone House (opposite). OVERLEAF Stone House is complemented by outbuildings—a barn on the left and garage/ greenhouse on the right—that make it a farm compound.

OUTBUILDINGS

POOL HOUSES

Pool houses satisfy a variety of needs, from concealing pumps and filters to accommodating changing rooms and spaces for entertaining. They also provide a visual focus or backdrop for the pool itself. In AR&T's hands pool houses range from simple background buildings to more fanciful follies. "Pool houses and outbuildings in general are less constrained by functional requirements than houses and are free to take almost any form."

At Stable House the changing rooms are attached to one side of the garage, which was sited to align with the axis of the existing pool. Like the garage and, indeed, the main house, the pool-changing-room wing is rendered in the vernacular of New England coastal farm outbuildings. Just inside the shuttered entrance to the wing, the clever recessed, diagonal entries to the changing rooms lend a dash of sophistication. Equally simple but more fanciful are The Cabanas, a pair of changing rooms that evoke the colorful striped tents on the beach at Biarritz. The stripes are clapboards laid vertically, instead of the more usual horizontal orientation, and cut at the bottom to form a sort of fringe.

The pool houses at Riverview House and Farm Villa are more commodious, even including living spaces and food-preparation areas. At Riverview House attenuated, stylized Ionic pilasters, a

reference to the Greek Revival vocabulary of the house, frame openings in the screened porch that occupies the central portion of the pool house. At Farm Villa the pool house presents a primitive, abstracted version of the Neoclassical language of the house and takes the form of a Greek stoa with simple heavy timber columns.

Katonah Pool House was converted from a derelict old icehouse. Weathered barn boards and rough-hewn beams were left exposed inside, lending character to the newly stylish living room. New doors and windows, including a trefoil "rose window," and board-and-batten siding give the exterior the flavor of a Gothic cottage. "This is a modest American version of the Gothic follies of grand English estates."

OPPOSITE, TOP A side wing of the Stable House garage faces the pool and includes a pair of changing rooms. OPPOSITE, BOTTOM The fanciful Cabanas evoke the colorful striped tents on the beach at Biarritz.
TOP At Farm Villa the pool house is a primitive version of a Greek stoa.
ABOVE The Gothic Katonah Pool House was converted from a derelict icehouse.

GUESTHOUSES, BARNS, AND POOL HOUSES

PLAYHOUSES AND GARDEN SHEDS

Garden sheds, like other outbuildings, can do more than serve a utilitarian purpose. "Villa Theresa" at Harbor Cottage and "DeVilla Delilah" at Long House are garden structures that double as playhouses named for the owner's granddaughters. Villa Theresa is child-size, barely tall enough for an adult to stand up in. The small-paned window helps establish a delicate scale. "When you see Villa Theresa from the main house, its small scale tricks you into thinking it is farther away and that the site is bigger than it really is." DeVilla Delilah accomplishes a similar optical illusion while also screening the garden from the neighbors. The symmetrical tool shed and playhouse pavilions are linked by a pergola that shelters facing benches in recessed alcoves. Small chimney-like towers rise from the pavilions as pedestals for four sculptures representing the seasons that belonged to the owner's grandmother.

The wood shed at Fishing Cabin holds a season's firewood but also helps define the space between the main cabin and a smaller guest cabin. The shed wraps around a south-facing deck, creating a pleasant, sunny place to sit on chilly mornings in the Catskills.

OPPOSITE, TOP A pergola links the playhouse and tool shed "pavilions" of DeVilla Delilah. OPPOSITE, BOTTOM Villa Theresa is a miniature playhouse/tool shed set in its own miniature, rabbit-proof garden. ABOVE The wood shed at Fishing Cabin doubles as the windbreak for a south-facing deck. OVERLEAF Like DeVilla Delilah, the Riverview House pool house consists of twin pavilions with a connector, in this case a screened porch.

SELECTED PROJECTS

1967

Pritchard's Cottage
Renovation
Bedford, NY

1968

Righter House Renovation
New Haven, CT

1969

Coolidge Camp,
with Sean Sculley
Squam Lake, NH

Spelman House,
with Peter Rose
Project, Cornwall Bridge, CT

LEFT At Little Camp rustic tree-trunk posts and rafter tails cut in the shape of fish heads frame the view from the porch out to the water.

1970

Vogue Foam Competition
Project

Motel, *with Peter Rose*
Project, Silverthorn, CO

1971

"Monitor House"
Oakes House
Fishers Island, NY

1972

Righter House Renovation
Noank, CT

Burwell Carriage House Renovation
New Haven, CT

Bald Peak Colony Club
Project, NH

1973

"Tower House"
Osborn House
Fishers Island, NY

Braun House
Fishers Island, NY

1975

Pearee Carriage House Renovation
New Haven, CT

Robinson House Renovation
Nonquitt, MA

1976

Killington Resort Hotel Competition,
with Carl Pucci
Project, Killington, VT

1977

Fisher House Renovation
Guilford, CT

"Cube House"
D. Johnson House
Fishers Island, NY

Climax Skateboard Park
Project, New Haven, CT

Robinson House Porch
Katonah, NY

Reynolds Aluminum Mobile Home
Mobil' Homme
Competition, *with Carl Pucci*

Half Mile Wall
Project, Earthwork
Bedford, NY

"Plot A" House
Project, Bedford, NY

1978

Cartwright House
Project, Bedford, NY

Dickinson House
Scotts Corners, NY

Japan Architect Competition
Shinkenchiku Residence

Van Hengel House
Fishers Island, NY

Old Connecticut State Capitol
Exhibition, Hartford, CT

O'Neill Playhouse-
on-the-Wharf
Competition, *with Andy Burr*
Provincetown, MA

Marshall House Renovation
Newtown, CT

1979

Fishers Island Country Club
Housing for Club Personnel
Fishers Island, NY

Fishers Island Country Club
Housing for Golf Club Personnel
Fishers Island, NY

Nelson House
Fishers Island, NY

P. Goss House
Project, Fishers Island, NY

Cook House
Project, Fishers Island, NY

Noyes House, *with Andy Burr*
Project, Fishers Island, NY

Locus House Addition
Essex, CT

Katonah Gallery Trompe l'Oeil Mural
Katonah, NY

Melbourne Landmark Competition,
with Carl Pucci

1980

Falk House
Nantucket, MA

Foley House
Nantucket, MA

Sperry House
Project, Bedford, NY

Colgate House
Project, Lloyd Harbor, NY

Righter House Renovation
Silver Eel Cove
Fishers Island, NY

"Atrium House"
Chase House
Project, Sanibel, Florida

Weld House Renovation and Additions 1980,1999
Essex, MA

Fishers Island Country Club
Condominiums
Project, Fishers Island, NY

Vietnam Veterans Memorial Competition
with Andy Burr, Carl Pucci

Righter Apartment Renovation
Pinckney St.
Boston, MA

Waterman Pool, Gallery
and Landscape
Project,
Fishers Island, NY

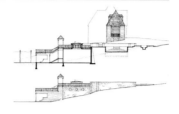

Northern Rose Realty Trust
82 Chestnut St. Apartment Building Renovation
Boston, MA

Northern Rose Realty Trust
Hancock St. Apartment Building Renovation
Boston, MA

Eagle Ridge Resort
Competition, CO

Evans House
Project, East Lyme, CT

Stedman House
Fishers Island, NY

"Gable in a Square"
Bogert House
Fishers Island, NY

Righter Office
58 Winter St.
Boston, MA

1982

Riegel House Renovation
Shingle Hill
Fishers Island, NY

Rhodes House Addition
Fishers Island, NY

Gardenway Competition
Pavilion of the Four Seasons

Brauns House Renovation
Project, Tuxedo Park, NY

Oakes Garage
Project, Fishers Island, NY

Andrews House Pavilions
Fishers Island, NY

"Keystone Cottage"
Hanes House
Fishers Island, NY

Boston Athenaeum Library Entry Proposal
Project, Boston, MA

Luce House Addition
Fishers Island, NY

"Arc Cottage"
Magowan House
Southampton, NY

Burnes House, 1982
Additions, 1995, 2000
Marstons Mills, MA

1983

"Fishing Cabin"
Whitman House, 1983
Woodshed Addition, 2003
Hardenbergh, NY

"Harbor Cottage"
Righter House
North Hill
Fishers Island, NY

Borland House
Fishers Island, NY

Wray House
Fishers Island, NY

Waterman Management Lena Building
Project, New London, CT

Fishers Island Fire House
Renovation and Addition, 1983, 2006
Project, Fishers Island, NY

Harvard Architectural
Review
Gate Competition
Cambridge, MA

Leach House
Project,
Attleboro, MA

1984

"Arcade House"
McConnaughey House
Southampton, NY

T. Kean House
Project, Fishers Island, NY

Copley Square Redevelopment
Competition, Boston, MA

Gordon House Renovations, 1984, 1996
Fishers Island, NY

Bogert House
Bedford, NY

"Pasture House"
Moody House, 1984
Addition, 1998
Fishers Island, NY

Andrews House
Project, Fishers Island, NY

Bailey House
Renovations, 1984,
1986, 1987, 1992, 2006
Fishers Island, NY

1985

Foshay House
Fishers Island, NY

Wilmerding Lodge Renovation
Fishers Island, NY

Wilmerding Paddock Renovation
Fishers Island, NY

Wilmerding Garage Renovation
Fishers Island, NY

Bonsal House Renovation
Fishers Island, NY

Kelland House Renovation
and Additions
Fishers Island, NY

"Garden Wall Cottage"
Berkowitz House
Fishers Island, NY

Zanghetti House Renovation & Addition
Fishers Island, NY

"Lantern Gate Lodge"
Wray Guest House
Fishers Island, NY

Bjork House
Norwalk, CT

Kibbe Studio Renovation
Fishers Island, NY

1986

Bailey Guest House
Renovation
Fishers Island, NY

"Family Camp"
Righter House, 1986
Dining Room Addition, 1999
North Haven, ME

Ellis House
Essex, MA

Steil House
Project,
Fishers Island, NY

"Island Tower"
Von Clemm House
North Haven, ME

Somerset Club Renovation
Boston, MA

Conant House
Fishers Island, NY

Connecticut Society
of Architects
Unbuilt Projects Competition
Farm Folly

Luce Power Plant
Fishers Island, NY

Barclay House
Project, Santa Fe, NM

1987

St. John's Church Renovations
Fishers Island, NY

Parrish Art Museum Bird House
Southampton, NY

Pierce/Rubenstein House
Project, Fishers Island, NY

L.M. Dalton
Co. House
(Washington
Ridge
Conservancy)
New Milford, CT

Baker House
Project,
Dubai, U.A.E.

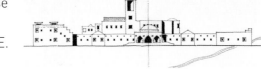

Skates House Renovation
Winchester, MA

Talbot House Renovation and Addition
North Salem, NY

1988

De Menil Caretaker's House
Fishers Island, NY

McLean House
Project,
Fishers Island, NY

Walsh Park Site Plan Proposals
Fishers Island, NY

Campbell House Renovation and Addition
Fishers Island, NY

J. L. Parsons House
Fishers Island, NY

Hermes of Paris
Boston, MA

Croll House Renovation and Addition
Chestnut Hill, MA

FIDCO Garage
Fishers Island, NY

Van Hengel Guest House
Fishers Island, NY

Boston Visions Competition
Boston, MA

Boston Visitors' Center Competition
Boston, MA

Thomas More College Library
Merrimack, NH

Thomas More College Chapel
Project, Merrimack, NH

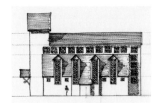

Strauss House
Project, Fishers Island, NY

1989

"The Cabanas"
Rothfeld Pool Houses
Fishers Island, NY

Brae Burn Country Club Pool House
Newton, MA

"Family Camp"
Righter Barn
The Sty
North Haven, ME

Shillo House
Fishers Island, NY

1990

Thomas More College Dormitory
Merrimack, NH

Marshall Guest House
North Haven, ME

Rutherfurd House
Project, Bedford, NY

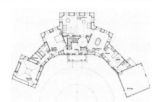

Coolidge House Renovation and Addition
Truro, MA

Fishers Island Beach Club Renovation
Fishers Island, NY

Portland "Gateway Gas"
Competition
Portland, ME

Hammond House Site Plan
Project, Marblehead, MA

1991

"Water House"
Ferguson House
Fishers Island, NY

Mockler/Sperry Guest House Renovation
Chatham, MA

Colloredo-Mansfeld Farmhouse Renovation
South Hamilton, MA

Wilmerding Pump House
Garden Folly
Project, Fishers Island, MA

"Cape Porch House"
Swartwood House
Cotuit, MA

"Cypress House"
Johnson/McKown House Renovation, 1991
Additions and Renovations, 1996, 1999, 2008
Milton, MA

Grossman House Renovation
Squam Lake, NH

"Checkerboard House"
Albert House
Cambridge, MA

"Temple House"
Estabrook Road House
Concord, MA

Cross House Renovation
Chicago, IL

Hicks House Renovation and Addition
Concord, MA

1992

Roosevelt House
Project, Chappaquiddick, MA

R. Parsons House Renovation and Addition
Fishers Island, NY

Righter
Woodland Chapel
North Haven, ME

Walker/Maysles House Addition
Fishers Island, NY

"Hillside House"
Thors House
Fishers Island, NY

V. F. Righter House Addition
Fishers Island, NY

"SeaBend"
Corn House, 1992
Addition, 2002
Sagamore Highlands, MA

Dean Carriage House Renovation
Marion, MA

Gary House Addition
Fishers Island, NY

Levinson House
Weston, MA

"Island Hill House"
P. Chapman House
Fishers Island, NY

1993

Guiney House
West Tisbury, MA

Wray House Addition
Fishers Island, NY

Augur House
Project, Aspen, CO

Lawrence Cabin I, 1993,
Cabin II, 1994
Boathouse, 2000
Vinalhaven, ME

"Pinwheel House"
Von Clemm Guest House/
Garage
North Haven, ME

Harvard Translations Office
Cambridge, MA

R. Tittmann/E. Sarda Apartment Renovation
Cambridge, MA

"Secret Garden House"
Robinson House
Northeast Harbor, ME

"Portico House"
Eisenberg House Addition
Cambridge, MA

1994

Lapsley House Renovation
Northeast Harbor, ME

Chambliss House
Chapoquoit, MA

Hunsaker Barn Renovation
Barnstable, MA

Trinity Church Sacristy
Cabinets
Boston, MA

Boston City Hall Plaza
Competition, Boston, MA

"Red House"
Clifford House
New Haven, VT

Sears House
Easton, NH

Augustine House
Stanfordville, NY

Evans House Addition
Lexington, MA

Reeve House Renovation
Concord, MA

Clifford Apartment Renovation
Cambridge, MA

1995

Lloyd House Porch
Sewanee, TN

Von Clemm Cabin
North Haven, ME

"The Shoebox"
Chafee House Addition
Sorrento, ME

R. Goss House Screened Porch Addition, 1995
Renovations, 1997
Fishers Island, NY

"Stable House"
Lofberg House Renovation
South Dartmouth, MA

"Stone House"
Macleod House
Medfield, MA

Grant Bookcase
Boston, MA

1996

Elias/Keane House Addition
Lincoln, MA

Newton Scientific, Inc., Offices
Cambridge, MA

"Penobscot Gable House"
Anderson/Cabot House
North Haven, ME

Nolen House Renovation
Great Island, MA

"Mews House"
Thorndike House
Brookline, MA

Lewis Garden Folly
Project, Sherborn, MA

1997

Becton House
Project, Blue Hill, ME

Leland House
Chappaquiddick, MA

Harding House Renovation
North Hall
York Harbor, ME

Johnson/McKown Barn
Milton, MA

Byrdhouse
Office Interior and Building Facade
Cambridge, MA

Ferguson Museum
Fishers Island, NY

R. Tittmann/ E. Sarda House Renovation and Addition
Belmont, MA

"Rotunda House"
J. Tittmann House
Cambridge, MA

1998

Harding House
North Haven, ME

Lawrence House Renovation
Chestnut Hill, MA

Phillips Trust Carriage House Renovation
Project, Salem, MA

"Farmyard House"
Schwarz House
Taghkanic, NY

Kohlenberg House
Westport, MA

Bernhard/Mayman House
Renovation and Addition
Andover, NH

"Riverview House"
Kaemmer House
Concord, MA

1999

Rifkind/Brandenburger House
Renovation
Cambridge, MA

Lewis Wharf
Project, Boston, MA

McLucas House Addition
Southwest Harbor, ME

McCall House, 1999, 2006
Project, Fishers Island, NY

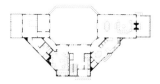

"Lake Library"
Grossman Library/Folly
Squam Lake, NH

Greenway Cabin
North Haven, ME

"Cape Courtyard House"
Corcoran House
Brewster, MA

Neilson House
Great Cranberry
Island, ME

Lawrence House
Vinalhaven, ME

2000

Clay Guesthouse/Barn
Ancramdale, NY

Pierce/Rubenstein Cabin
Renovations and House Additions
Fishers Island, NY

Johnson/Ketterson House Renovation
Osterville, MA

Hamblett House
Project,
South Dartmouth, MA

"Cape Tower House"
Clay House
Great Island, MA

Johnson Union Wharf Renovation
Boston, MA

Frisco Housing Development
Frisco, TX

2001

"Winnepocket House"
Phillips House
Webster, NH

Williams House Renovation
and Addition
Wellesley, MA

"Rocksyde"
Cross House
Manchester, MA

Warren House Renovation
(H.H. Richardson House)
Project, Brookline, MA

Sorrento Library Renovation
Project, Sorrento, ME

"Six Gables"
Colloredo-Mansfeld House
South Hamilton, MA

Hodges Apartment Renovation
Boston, MA

"Island House"
R. Parsons House
Fishers Island, NY

Watson House
North Haven, ME

2002

Heavner Spec House
Wellesley, MA

Cashman House
Project, Chester,
Nova Scotia

"Mountaintop House"
Clark/Porter House
Northeast Harbor, ME

Hodge Boiler Works
DeNormandie Wharf
Project, Boston, MA

"Farm Villa"
Von Moltke House, 2002,
Garage Apartment, 2005,
Pool House, 2006
Hartford, VT

Ames Free Library Tower Restoration
North Easton, MA

Casino
Project, Biddeford, ME

2003

Johnson House Renovation
Osterville, MA

Johnson Game House
Project, Mt. Desert, ME

J. Kean House Renovation
Fishers Island, NY

Berk House Addition,
with Sally Berk
Indian Lake, NY

Macleod House Renovation
Fishers Island, NY

Ware House
Barnstable, MA

Riegel House Renovation
Hay Harbor Golf Course
Fishers Island, NY

New Jerk City
Competition
with Carl Pucci

2004

Whitman Guest Cabin
Catskills, NY

"Long House"
Righter House Renovation
and Additions,
with Libby Turowski
Mattapoisett, MA

"Farm Cottage"
Hunnewell/Kaplan House
Wellesley, MA

Righter Earthwork
North Haven, ME

Robinson House
Hilltop
Project, Cornwall, CT

2005

"Little Camp"
Bennett House
Edgartown, MA

North Haven
Historical Society
North Haven, ME

Louisburg Farm Barn
Wellington, FL

Coolidge Camp II
Squam Lake, NH

Albright/Bernstein House
Brookline, MA

Sibble House Renovation
Milton, MA

2006

Robinson House Renovation
Treetop
Cornwall, CT

Costin House Addition
Nahant, MA

2007

D. Chapman House
Project, Middletown, RI

O'Leary House Renovation and Addition
Marion, MA

Stanley House
North Stonington, CT

Johnson/Ketterson House Renovation and Addition
Project, Tremont, ME

Hoyt Boathouse
South Dartmouth, MA
MA

Harvard Lampoon Renovation
Cambridge, MA

Longfellow House Pergola
Cambridge, MA

2008

Johnson/McKown
Tennis House
Milton, MA

Milton Academy Lower School
Admissions Office Renovation
Milton, MA

Dedham Community Theatre Marquee
Dedham, MA

Smith House Renovation
Boston, MA

Biemann House
Cambridge, MA

Swan Boat Pavilion
Competition
Boston, MA

2009

Woburn Library Competition
Woburn, MA

Woburn Library Competition
J. Righter & C. Pucci Entry
Woburn, MA

Milton Academy
Headmaster's House Renovation
Milton, MA

ALBERT, RIGHTER & TITTMANN: THE TEAM, PAST AND PRESENT

(Principals' names are in boldface)

Jim Righter

Patrick Hickox

Heather MacIsaac

Sheldon Whitehouse

Jacob Albert

Brigid Williams

Sandy Righter

Michael Paplow

Frank Cheney

Michael Paplow

R. T. Lyman

Kim Lovejoy

Lisa Gray

Marc duBois

Terry Dwan

Chris Wolfe

Craig Gibson

Kimo Griggs

Hetty Smith

Alec Stuart

Andrew Garthwaite

Stefanie von Clemm

L.T. Thorn

Cynthia Wardell

David Robinson

Jeff Dalzell

Andy Bernheimer

Brooke Trivas

Jennifer Warr

Nick Iselin

Carrie Hamilton

Susanna Horton

Lisa Powers

John Tittmann

Mark Myers

David Guarino

Matthew Littell

Gabriel Stadecker

Kate Lemos

Craig Gibson

Christine Finn

Gigi Saltonstall

Jenny Ford Barrett

Sarah Felton

Sally Curtis

David Cutler

Lisa Walbridge

Lyssa Castonguay

Willy Ulbrich

McMillan West Doherty

August Ventimiglia

Katie Elliott

J.B. Clancy

Laura Shea

Clio Chafee

Andrew Wenrick

William Truslow

Karen Kim

Lyle Bradley

Heidi Cron

George de Brigard

Justin Finnicum

Kreh Mellick

Julie Lynch

Eric Rochon

Michelle Bureau Koch

Mieke Stethem

Aaron Helfand

Jonathan Dowse

Abigail Lewis

Julie Zelermyer

Lisa Lombardi

D.J. Arthur

Emilie Pickering

Lee Elsey

Mary Burr

ASSOCIATED ARCHITECTS:

Sean Sculley

Peter Rose

Andy Burr

Carl Pucci

ACKNOWLEDGMENTS

First off, I'd like to thank Jacob Albert, Jim Righter, and John Tittmann; it's truly been a delight to work with them and see their houses. I treasured every moment we spent together, whether in their offices in Boston or individually in their respective homes.

I'd also like to thank my editor, Jackie Decter, for her patience and guidance, Sarah Davis for her kind words, and the rest of the staff at The Vendome Press. Then, of course, there are my parents and my partner, Andrea, to whom I am indebted for their support.

I also owe a huge debt to Clio Chafee, without whose incredible organizational skills this project would not have been possible. Her passing away in the midst of our efforts was a tremendous blow, and it grieves me that I never got the chance to tell her how wonderful she was.

And finally, I'd like to thank Witold Rybczynski, who doesn't know me from Adam, but whose work has been an inspiration to me, for it showed me that writing about architecture can be lively and enriching.

DAN COOPER

This book would not have been possible without the excellent work of the photographers whose pictures are featured and without the enthusiasm and efforts of Mark Magowan, Jackie Decter, and Sarah Davis at The Vendome Press. We had great fun working with Dan Cooper in finding a way to express what our work means.

We gratefully acknowledge the inspiration and support of family and mentors. We thank our clients for giving us such wonderful opportunities. We value the collaboration of all who have worked with us in the office and of engineers, landscape architects, and interior designers. We thank our accountant and advisor, Tim O'Toole, and, most of all, Sandy Righter for encouraging us to pursue this book.

JIM RIGHTER, JACOB ALBERT, AND JOHN TITTMANN

PHOTO & ILLUSTRATION CREDITS

Peter Aaron ESTO: pp. 29 bottom, 71 bottom row right, 76–77 top row left, 106–7 bottom row left

Robert Benson: pp. 1, 2, 6, 8, 22–23, 25, 26–27, 32, 34–35, 36, 38, 39, 44, 45 bottom, 50, 51, 52–53, 54 left and right, 55, 56–57 top row right, middle row second from left and second from right, bottom row second from left, 58, 60, 63 top and bottom, 66, 67, 76–77 top row second from right, bottom row second from left and second from right, 81 top and bottom, 82, 88 top right and bottom, 89 left and right, 97 left, 98–99 4a and 4b, 6a and 6b, 106 top, 106–7 top row left and second from left, 113 top and bottom, 114, 116, 117, 119, 120, 121, 123, 126 top, 127 right, 128, 130–31 top row left, center, and right, middle row right, bottom row left and second from left, 134, 138, 139, 142, 143, 144, 146–47, 148, 151, 152, 156–57 top row left, second from left, and right, bottom row second from left and second from right, 158, 161 top and bottom left, 162, 166, 168, 169, 172 top and bottom, 178–79, 180, 182–83, 190 left, 191, 192–93, 194 top, 195 top, 198–99

Erik Borg: pp. 56–57 bottom row second from right, 108–9, 129

David Cutler: p. 43 bottom (watercolor)

Lisa Lombardi: p. 161 bottom right (watercolor)

Sam Ogden: pp. 96, 149, 150, 167

Greg Premru: pp. 16, 61 top and bottom, 106–7 middle row right, 118, 122 left, 132, 137 left and right, 145 bottom, 174 left, 185

Nat Rea: pp. 127 left, 130–31 middle row second from left, 156–57 middle row second from left, 176–77, 196 top

Chip Riegel: pp. 12–13, 42–43 top, 42 bottom, 76–77 top row second from left and right, 98–99 2a and 2b

Steve Rosenthal: pp. 14, 20, 21

Eric Roth: p. 163

Evan Sklar: pp. 56–57 middle row right, 97 right, 135, 153, 170

Brian Vanden Brink: pp. 4, 9 top, 40, 41 top and bottom, 48, 49 left and right, 78, 84, 85, 88 top right and bottom, 89 left and right, 92, 93, 94–95, 103, 106–7 middle row center, 110, 124, 125, 130–31 middle row second from right, 140, 141, 145 top, 154, 155, 156–57 bottom row left, 164, 175, 200–201

Judith Watts: pp. 56–57 top row second from left, 101, 122 right

Nick Wheeler: pp. 31, 46–47, 98–99 5a and 5b, 104–5, 112, 130–31 bottom row second from right, 186

PAGE 1: The front door at Rocksyde opens from an unassuming shingled exterior into a gleaming rotunda that reorients you and leads to the interiors beyond.

PAGE 2: With its broad roof overhang and low walls that extend past the house, Farmyard House reaches out to the landscape.

PAGE 4: At Little Camp a small study alcove with a panoramic view has a ribbed-wood ceiling that is reminiscent of the hull of a boat.

First published in the United States of America in 2009 by
The Vendome Press
1334 York Avenue
New York, NY 10021
www.vendomepress.com

ISBN 978-0-86565-253-8

Editor: Jacqueline Decter
Photo Editor: Sarah Davis
Designers: Joel Avirom and Jason Snyder

Library of Congress Cataloging-in-Publication Data

Cooper, Dan (Daniel Robert), 1958–
  New classic American houses : the architecture of Albert, Righter &Tittmann / text by Dan Cooper ; foreword by Robert A.M. Stern.
    p. cm.
  Includes index.
  ISBN 978-0-86565-253-8
  1. Albert, Righter & Tittmann. 2. Architecture, Domestic—United States.
  I. Title.
  NA737.A39C66 2009
  728.0973—dc22
                                                    2009007810

Printed by Toppan Printing Co., Ltd., in China
First printing